National Trust Neptune (

Launched in 1956 it aims to:

- Alert people to the pressure facing underde
- Acquire and own unspoilt coastline for permanent preservation of paths and public access
- Show the benefits of protection by the National Trust
- Raise money for new coastal purchases, their endowment and repair

Today the National Trust protects about 20% of the coastline of England and Wales, (Scotland has its own National Trust). This enables residents and visitors alike to enjoy the county's coastal path - from harbours to inlets, on beaches or along rocky cliffs.

Through the efforts of the Neptune Coastal Campaign, the National Trust is working to protect estuaries, such as the Fal in Cornwall and the Yealm in Devon. Important maritime sites survive because they are in the care of the Trust, such as the beautiful harbour of Boscastle in Cornwall.

When the National Trust takes on a length of coastline, it tries to protect the whole landscape that forms the backdrop to the seashore. Often this involves buying the land as far inland as the skyline. That means over 125,000 acres of land is protected. In Devon, a spectacular stretch of coastline between Wembury and Salcombe demonstrates how the Trust can build up the protection of an area gradually, by purchasing small areas of coastal land as they become available.

Walkers may wish to find out more about the National Trust from *The National Trust in Devon* leaflets obtainable in most information centres These leaflets contain information on walking trails as well as local history, flora, fauna, places on interest.

What can you do to help?

If you would like to make a contribution towards the vital work of the Neptune Campaign, you can do so by calling the National Trust Donations Hotline on 0208 315 111 or get on line to www.nationaltrust.org.uk/coastline to find out more.

THE NATIONAL TRUST

Alternatively, you could write to:
Neptune Coastline Campaign
The National Trust
Killerton House, Broadclyst
Exeter EX5 3LE.

NEPTUNE COASTLINE CAMPAIGN

Thanks and Acknowledgements

I would like to thank all of those who gave me their help and took the time to provide information and the contributors named in the text. Of those, I would like to mention Cynthia Thomas for her unfailing support and encouragement, Bobbie Blackler of Plymouth Yacht Haven, Helen Deaves of Stanfords Charts, Mike Hooton of Weir Quay Boatyard, Commodore Don Macrae of Plym Yacht Club, Mike Morris of National Coastwatch Institution, Robert Newton of Looe and Edward Webb- Looe Harbour Master, Robin Page of Mayflower International Marina, Julian Stapely- River Yealm Harbour Master, and Vanessa Tabb of Salcombe Harbour Authority. The following copyright material has been used, with permission, in this book: Certain photographs from Bridgend Boat Company Ltd, Joan Gross, National Coastwatch Institution, Mayflower International Marina, The National Trust, Plymouth Yacht Haven, Weir Quay Boatyard. Tide Tables provided by kind permission of the UK Hydrographer, extracts from Charts 13 provided by kind permission of Stanford Charts.

Other Books by the author

South African Nautical Almanac
2002/2003, 5th Edition ISBN 0-620-29310-6 On Board Publications

Afloat & Ashore 1
Falmouth, Fowey and Helford Rivers 2002/2003 ISBN 0-09541900-1-7
On Board Publications

South Atlantic Circuit (in preparation)
In collaboration with the RCC Pilotage Foundation ISBN0-9541900-3-3
On Board Publications

Afloat & Ashore 2000/2001
A pilot guide to the Fal & Helford estuaries ISBN 0-9541900-1-7
On Board Publications

Boat Trekkers Guide
1998 (with Sue Morgan) ISBN 0-949989-71-1
SA Yachting

Afloat & Ashore 2

Start Point to Looe 2002/2003

A Boating Guide to Plymouth, Salcombe and the River Yealm

Tom Morgan MRIN

Series Editor: Sue Morgan

Any matters relating to this production must be referred to the publishers, On Board Publications.

Foreword

Thank you for buying a copy of the first edition of *Afloat & Ashore* 2002/2003- a small craft pilot guide toPlymouth, Salcombe, and River Yealm. As well as sailing directions there is a marine trades directory and listing. Certain quality shoreside services and facilities are also included.

This book covers one of England's most superb sailing grounds. The accessible coastline of South Devon is unique. I hope that it does not become scarred by modern development retail blocks like so many places worldwide. There is deep water sailing for the larger yacht or many creeks and quiet stretches of rivers for those looking for solitude. As a newcomer, I have had great fun and enjoyment discovering the joys of Salcombe, and the rivers in this book. I consider myself very fortunate to have received so much help and advice. This has been largely due to the assistance from professionals and amateurs involved in all aspects of waterside life. Also, it has enabled me to have much of the text verified before publication.

My thanks must go to the individual advertisers who put their faith in me to publish the first edition of this book. I would encourage readers to support them in their enterprises. They recognized the need for a cost-effective local sailing guide and their sponsorship should be applauded.

ISBN 0-9541900-2-5

Printed in Cornwall by Booths (Bookbinder) Ltd. of Mabe.

On Board Publications.
Address: 123 Canberra Towers
Southampton SO19 9JX
Telephone: 07787-150-339
Email: onboardpublications@hotmail.com

Contents

Distance Planner

Many channel cruises use Start Point as a point of departure, and traditionally as a landfall. Whilst GPS has taken uncertainty out of knowing your position, I have been encouraged to include a distance planner. The destinations and distances are listed from east to west. There is no attempt to cover all possible routes. All distances are approximate, in sea miles, and are from 5 miles off Start Point to open water off the destination. It is the navigator's responsibility to ensure the safety of the craft.

Start Point to:

Needles Fairway Buoy	80
Portland Bill	54
Cherbourg	83
Alderney	63
Guernsey, Little Russell	58
Guernsey, Les Hanois Lt.	56
Jersey	88
St. Malo	106
River Trieux	80
River Treguier	78
Roscoff	88
L'Aberwrach	100
Le Four Channel	118
Falmouth	55
Lizard	68
Scillies	112

Local Maritime Radio Broadcast Schedules
Navigation Warnings and Weather Bulletins

Station: Brixham Coastguard MRSC

Location: King's Quay, Brixham,
Devon TQ59 9TW
Tel: 01803-882704 Fax: 01803-882780
Geographical Position: 50º 24'N 03º 31'W
DSC: MMSI 002320013,
DSC: VHF Channel 70
Calling Channel: (R/T) VHF Channel 16
R/T Working VHF Channels:
VHF Ch 73 East of River Exe
VHF Ch 10 from Prawle Point

Bulletins are read on the broadcast channels below after an announcement on VHF Channel 16 in the following order:

A Navigation Warnings - UK Sea Regions Delta and Foxtrot
B Shipping Forecast for areas Plymouth and Portland
C Gale Warnings for areas above*
D Inshore Forecast, for up to 12 miles offshore
E Strong wind warnings if in force (over Force 6)
F M.O.D. Range Information

GMT	0050	0450	0850	1250	1650	2050
A	VHF	VHF	VHF	VHF	VHF	VHF
B			VHF			VHF
C	VHF	VHF	VHF	VHF	VHF	VHF
D	VHF	VHF	VHF	VHF	VHF	VHF
E	VHF	VHF	VHF	VHF	VHF	VHF
F	VHF	VHF	VHF	VHF	VHF	VHF

There is an outlook given after weather bulletins
*At times of issue as well as when in force

BBC Radio 4 Shipping Forecasts

All times are clock times.
Variations from 0535 schedule: Saturday 0542, Sunday 0556

TIME	0048	0535	1201	1754
	LW	LW	LW	LW
	MW	MW		
	VHF	VHF		

Key: LW is 198 kHz (AM), MW is 720 kHz (AM)
VHF is 92.4 to 94.6 MHz (FM) (97.1MHz in the Channel Islands)
Inshore Waters forecasts are given after the 0048 and 0535 bulletins.
These are usually valid until 1800 that day.

National Coastwatch Institution
Prawle Point Station, Tel: 01548-551259
Rame Head Station, Tel: 01752- 823706
One can telephone the station for a current weather forecast, during daylight hours..
The watch keeper may be able to advise on local conditions.

BBC Radio Devon Inshore Weather Forecasts

NOTE: Bulletins may be after news and announcements.

All times are clock times and are only approximate. It is advised to listen some minutes before these times.

Inshore Weather forecasts

Weekdays	0530	0605	0833	1330	1735
Saturdays		0605	0833	1305	
Sundays		0605	0833	1305	

Coastal Conditions including Shipping and Tides may be given at these times.

Frequencies:
VHF F.M. in MHz: 94.8, 94.8, 96.0, 103.4
MW A.M. in kHz: 801, 855, 990, 1458

Useful telephone numbers not listed elsewhere in this book.

Accident & Emergency	01752 792511
Coach Enquiries	0990 808080
Environment Agency	0800 807060
National Coastwatch Institution	01548 511259
Post Office Enquiries	0345 223344
H.M. Customs (Duty Officer)	01752 234600
Rail Enquiries	08457 484950
Radio Devon	01752 260323
Tourist Information	01752 266030
Western Morning News	01752 203232

NAVTEX and World Wide Web

Although a local guide, this NAVTEX information has been included as it is the single most helpful means worldwide of receiving shipping forecasts, navigational warnings and M.O. D. notices of activity. Although there are four hourly broadcasts scheduled, relevant station and times of messages are below. (Weather forecast times are in bold.) In the area covered by this book your equipment will receive other stations. The dedicated receiver on 518 kHz needs no operator input after initial set-up. One can choose which types of messages to record either on screen or on paper. There is a listing below. Gale warnings are issued on receipt and then incorporated into the schedule.

Station	ID	Times (U.T.C.)					
Niton	S	0300	**0700**	1100	1500	**1900**	2300

Subjects of Messages

A	Coastal Navigation Warnings
B	Gale Warnings
C	Ice Reports
D	Initial Distress Information
E	Weather Messages
F	Pilot Service Message
G	Electronic NAVAID Information
L	NAVAREA Warning
Z	QRU (No message on hand)

U RL for Shipping Forecast

For those with access to the Web you can receive the latest Shipping Forecast direct from the Meteorological Office web site, without going to the home page. It can be found on the following address, http://www.meto.gov.uk/datafiles/offshore.html.

Safety First and Last

The sea and weather show no respect to people. Did you know that a large number of male bodies recovered by the US Coast Guard have their trouser flies open! So be aware at all times. The UK Coastguard service is part of the Marine and Coastguard Agency. The members are there to help. You can help by donating to the Royal National Lifeboat Institution. Write to RNLI, West Quay Road, Poole, Dorset BH15 1HZ or look in the local telephone book.

Some things to do before setting out by boat

- Check the weather using the information in the Weather Information Pages on 0891-505-200 or Teletext 188 and 205
- Make sure you have enough fuel - and some for contingencies.
- Ensure the engine is in good running order and bring your tool kit and spares.
- Make an equipment check that everything is working properly
- Use the relevant charts and **check the tides**. It takes a lot longer against the wind and tide
- Plan your trip.**Make sure someone knows when you are expected to arrive back.**
- Join the voluntary Yacht and Boat Safety Scheme. It's **free**. Contact your local Coastguard on 01803-882704 for details.
- Get some training in safety, radio working (MAYDAY, etc.) and navigation.
- Make sure your flares are in date and your radar reflector can be hoisted in the correct attitude

Some things you should do out there

- Make sure there is an approved life jacket for everyone on board and wear them if conditions deteriorate.
- Wear warm and **windproof** clothing and **sunglasses** when appropriate.
- Insist that everyone knows what to do in a man overboard situation. **It could be you** that goes in
- Make sure that you are not the only one who knows how to operate the radio. **Get an annual licence for the boat and an operators certificate for yourself.**
- Carry an alternative means of propulsion **and a towrope**. Do not risk it with only one engine out at sea.
- Keep a good lookout at all times.
- Be sensible about drinking. It can impair your judgement.

Some things to do if conditions deteriorate

- Do not press on regardless, try to seek shelter immediately.
- If in doubt call for help. Many people leave it too late and a problem escalates into a life-threatening crisis. It's easier to find you in daylight than at night.

Start Point to Plymouth

Charts: Imray C5 and C6 (from Prawle Point) Stanfords 13 BA 1613 BA SC5602

Start Point

Start Point was a welcome sight for Royal Navy sailing ship captains running east for their winter anchorage of Torbay before a gale. Today, skippers of most leisure craft round it to the west with peaceful intentions. The Fl.W. (3) 10 sec. light at 62metres in position 50°13.3´N 03°38.5´W in the unmistakable white tower looks out over the detached rocks that extend some way southward. The overfalls can extend almost a mile south in strong wind and the full spring tide. One commercial pilot book states it is possible to avoid the overfalls by passing close to the rocks during daytime. The advice is to give the area at least a mile offing in such conditions. Passing this headland the rate and direction of the tide are major considerations. At springs in strong westerly winds, it can reach 4 knots. The effect of the Race is much less three miles south. According to the locals, the tide turns east 2 hours before high water Plymouth, and west about four and a half hours after. In settled weather craft waiting for a change of tide could anchor in Lannacombe Bay just west of Start Point

Craft coming from Dartmouth or the 'Riviera' can cheat the tide by staying close to the shore of Start Bay and coming out into the stream only to clear Start Rocks to continue westwards. Once well south of the land, say south of latitude 50º11´N, Falmouth is about 55 miles away on a course just south of west (265º). On this course one will leave the Eddystone light, Fl (2)10 sec. 20M about a mile to the north. The fixed red sector over Hands Deep, to the northwest of the Eddystone Rocks, will not be seen on this direct course.

Lannacombe Bay

Prawle Point NCI Station, Joan Gross

About three and a half miles west-southwest of the Start along the cliffs is Prawle Point. The old white coast guard station is back in use with the National Coastwatch Institution. Once past, The Range opens out to starboard. In the northwest of the bay is Salcombe. See later for approaches to this sunken ria. Craft heading west can shape a course to round Bolt Head about 3 miles further on just north of west. Bolt Tail is some 5 miles northwest further along the cliffs.

The latter surmounted by a disused coast guard lookout marks the start of seven mile long Bigbury Bay. Hope Cove, where there has been increased modern building, nestles behind Bolt Tail. It is a daytime anchorage in winds from north-northeast to south in depths of 10 to 2 metres. Run in on a course keeping the old coast guard station on a bearing 110º. Beware the drying Basses Rocks inshore and the lobsterpot buoys. This is a good place for shallow draft craft waiting for the tide to enter the River Avon. This shallow river entrance is hidden from the north behind Burgh Island. Approach to the river should only be made from south of the island as there is little water shoreward and northward of the island. Some craft anchor east of Murray's Rocks whilst waiting for the tide. The modernistic hotel, on the shoreward side, is where Agatha Christie wrote some of her books. The charm of this area has changed little since, and it is often used as a film location up to this day.

Continuing across the bay the River Erme will be seen on the starboard hand as craft continue north-northwest to clear Hillsea Point. Hillsea Point Rock and the shallow patch further on, should be left to starboard. Keep in over 24 metres rounding Hillsea Point and shape a course to pass Wembury Bay towards the 58-metre high Great Mew Stone Rock. The latter can be seen from afar and is a good guide for craft heading directly for Plymouth ensuring it is left to the northeast. Inshore of the Great Mew Stone is Wembury Point and the

Prawle Point from eastward

Gunnery Range. The unlit yellow buoys marking the target area on uncorrected charts have been removed. Live firing was due to cease in August 2001.Consult the GUNFACTS on NAVTEX and listen to navigational warnings from the Coast Guard. See 'Local Maritime Radio' later.

The yellow target buoys on older charts- NGS West and NGS East in about 50°11′N and near latitude 04°00′W were on a direct course from Prawle Point to Falmouth. They are also due to be removed.

Keep south of 50°18′N until well west of 04°05′W to avoid Ebb Rocks before making for the River Yealm, if that is your destination. The best visual guide is to keep the bearing of the Plymouth Western Breakwater light tower greater than 305°. The breakwater tower will be seen in transit with the shoreward edge of Great Mew Stone. (See later for River Yealm.)

Giving the Great Mew Stone a half a mile offing will bring craft up to Plymouth Sound. Although it is left at a lesser distance by the locals, do not be tempted to pass shoreward of the rocks. There is no passage. One should avoid the Tinker bank off the Shagstone beacon; its ends are marked with an east and west cardinal buoy respectively. Finally, head for the eastern entrance marked with a L.Fl.WR 10 sec. light on the eastern end of the Plymouth Breakwater in position 50°20′N 04°08.3′W. For approaches to Plymouth, see later.

Great Mewstone

Salcombe

Known to be the subject of Tennyson's *Crossing the Bar* and trotted out in so many pilot books, the natural barrier has not deterred the floating holiday maker/cruiser. So many craft are moored (or anchored) cruising yachts are not permitted to sail within the harbour during July and August. Nowadays, it is a popular stopover for people working their way along the coast in easy stages. Exiting on the last half of the flood favours those craft heading east whilst those heading west can leave near high water. There is an increasing number of trailable craft launching from the slip in Gould Road.

Called the Salcombe River by many, the sunken ria was too remote to be totally affected by 'modern progress'. During the winter the resident population is greatly reduced because much of the accommodation is now holiday apartments, B & B's and hotels. The town has numerous cafes and restaurants where you can eat and drink. The bed & breakfast sector is growing, as is the organization of the Harbour Master. The harbour staff are coping with an ever-increasing number of craft. There is always the hope of those paying harbour dues, that some of those funds collected will be designated into the budget for

Biddlehead

building ablution facilities for yachtsmen, by the next edition of this book.

One of the delights of a visit to Salcombe is a visit to the Chocolate Factory. It is set at the Shadycombe end of Island Street. The raised seating area outside leads to a chocoholic dream and a must for visitors looking for that something, a little bit different. The shop is stocked with all things chocolate. Upstairs there is a glass-fronted viewing area where one can get a rare treat – the chance to see hand-made chocolate being made, and ask the chocolatier questions over the audio-link. The best Belgian manufacturer, Callebaut, supplies all of the raw chocolate.

Approach

To quote *Sailing Days* by Adlard Coles, writing in 1944: "Salcombe Harbour right from the entrance to its upper reaches is a lovely picture. It is a gem set in a massive setting. On the approach from the west stands the Mewstone backed by Bolt Head and to the east the formidable cliff line extending to the Prawle." The jagged cliffs either side have a starkness split only by the buildings in the western end the town. One should keep off the east shore to avoid the Chapple Rocks and head for the western side of the entrance before closing the bar.

Craft from the west may anchor in Starehole Bay but need to keep clear of the wreck in the northwest corner. Rounding Bolt Head and the Mewstone at more than two cables distant the town will appear. During May to September a buoy (yellow) is in position off the southeastern corner. This should be left to port before heading for the gap ahead. Once the town is in sight aim to clear Great Eelstone by at least a cable. At certain times the procession of yachts, in or out, will be your best guide.

Anchored off Portlemouth

Craft approaching from the east will see two groups of gabled houses, both reddish in hue. This could be confusing to the first timer, especially as most pilot books only mention one. (The second is set back towards the top of North Sand Bay and not visible when rounding from the west). It is the more easterly of the two that is just to the east of the leading line over the bar. See colour photograph page 10. One should keep off the east shore to avoid the Chapple Rocks and head for the western side of the Range before closing the bar.

The bar should be approached when there is sufficient water. With one metre charted depth at LAT, navigators are reminded to ensure that this condition is met. From observation, craft do come and go most of the time in settled weather and local information from harbour staff claimed at least 2 metres depth at LW neaps. This was confirmed by soundings (August 2001). Salcombe high water is about the same time as H.W. Plymouth, or up to ten minutes after. The ebb and a fresh onshore wind can create tricky conditions. First time visitors should avoid these. If there is any uncertainty try calling *Salcombe Harbour* on VHF Channel 16/14. The harbour staff is known to be very accommodating and there is always someone to help from 0600 – 2200 from mid-May to mid-September.

Entry

This is best when depths are greater than half-tide. The leading line is on 000°. The forward mark on Pound Stone Rock is a red/white pole topped by a red diamond. It is difficult to distinguish from the other red/white poles marking the port hand side of the channel after entry. Behind this is the leading sectored light on the red/white pole topped by a diamond. The double-gabled house appearing to the east of the rear mark will help identification. The RWG 2 sec. range 7 miles shows red to port (west) and green to starboard (east) of the safe white sector 357° - 002°. Neither is easy to see from offshore by day but the light of the rear mark is easy to identify at night in clear conditions. A fellow visitor who

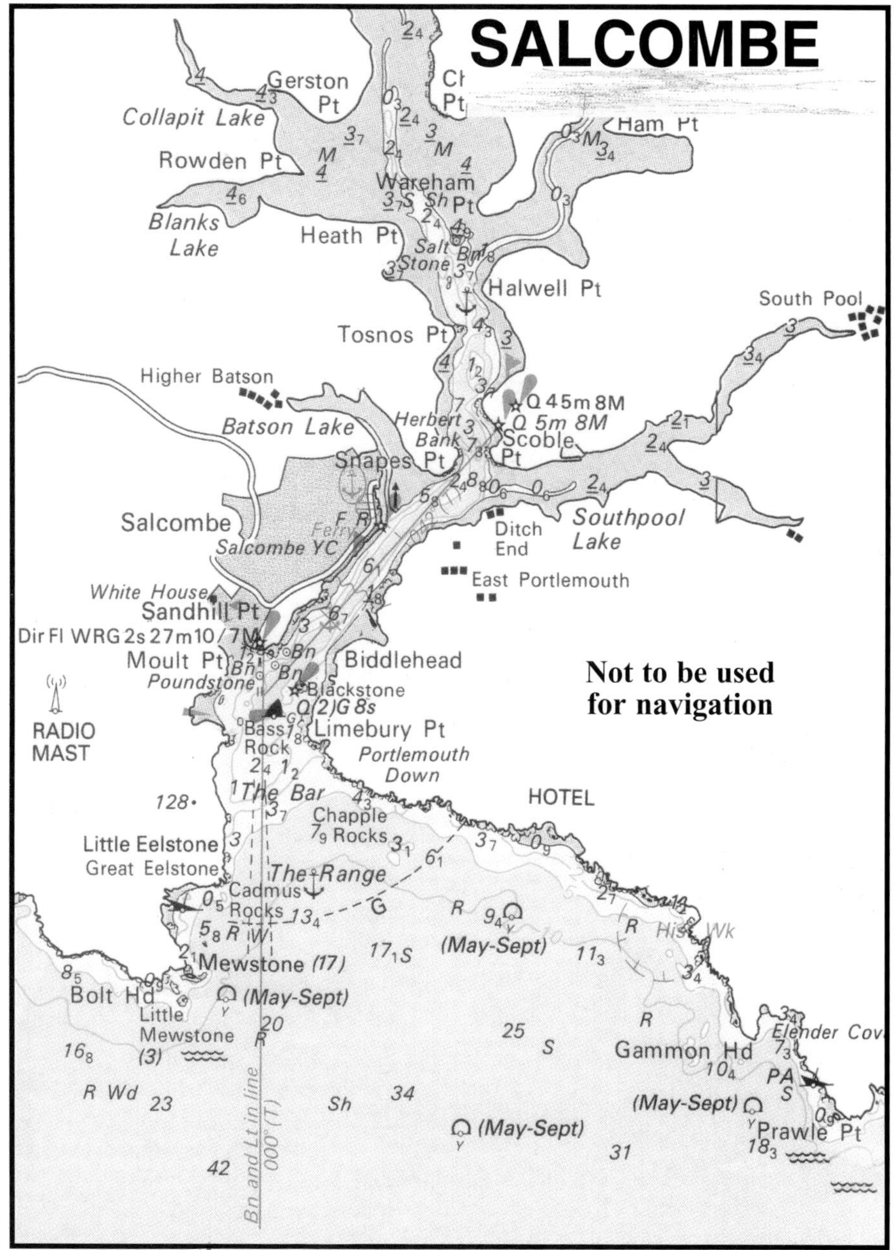
SALCOMBE
Not to be used for navigation
Gerston Pt
Collapit Lake
Rowden Pt
Blanks Lake
Heath Pt
Wareham Pt
Salt Stone
Halwell Pt
Ham Pt
South Pool
Tosnos Pt
Higher Batson
Batson Lake
Herbert Bank
Snapes Pt
Scoble Pt
Q 45m 8M
Q 5m 8M
Salcombe
Salcombe YC
Ferry
Ditch End
Southpool Lake
East Portlemouth
White House
Sandhill Pt
Dir Fl WRG 2s 27m10/7M
Moult Pt
Poundstone
Biddlehead
Blackstone
Q(2)G 8s
Bass Rock
Limebury Pt
Portlemouth Down
RADIO MAST
The Bar
HOTEL
Chapple Rocks
Little Eelstone
Great Eelstone
The Range
Cadmus Rocks
Mewstone (17)
(May-Sept)
Bolt Hd
Little Mewstone (3)
R His Wk
Gammon Hd
Elender Cov
Prawle Pt
Bn and Lt in line 000°(T)

brought his boat in during darkness for the first time confirmed the ease of a night entrance, though during the entry he was concerned that the leading line took the craft in close to the cliffs on the western side of the Ridge. When making a night entry, the Q.Fl. lights, just north of Scoble Point will guide craft towards the Bag.

Once you have entered, craft should turn to starboard leaving Bass Rock to port. Wolf Rock Q.G. buoy and Blackstone Rock Q.G. (2) 8sec. light, range 2 miles should be left to starboard. By now Scoble Point Light will guide craft into at least 5 metres. During the season the anchored larger craft and the light of the town will assist orientation. Beacons mark the channel up towards Woodville Rocks. From there craft can head for the moorings. Large Scale Stanford Chart 22 or Imray Chart Y48 are recommended.

Salcombe Harbour

Harbour Master
Salcombe Harbour Authority
Harbour Office
Whitestrand Street
Salcombe TQ8 8BU
Tel: 01548 843791
Fax: 01548 842033
Email: salcombe.harbour@south-hams-dc.gov.uk

One should not anchor until past Biddlehead with its charted disused slip and the electricity cable signposted with diamond topped beacons. In the summer, the bays on the southern side of the harbour have substantial dinghy sailing facilities. There are visitors' moorings past this point in front of the Salcombe

Salcombe Yawls

Yacht Club and the Marine Hotel. These yellow and orange buoys are marked 'visitors'. As one proceeds there are more moorings on the edge of the fairway. Some pilot books claim anchorage is possible here, although rafting up to a mooring is the norm. A good spot to find anchorage is just past the ferry landing on the East Portlemouth side. It gets crowded in the summer, so one cannot guarantee peace or solitude. One hazard at this popular destination is the "learner dinghy".

Moorings off Snapes Point

Note: On the last day of Regatta in August, a flotilla of boats that includes some large fishing vessels plies up and down the harbour at a rapid speed. Occupants of these craft hurl water bombs and hoses are turned on people apparently indiscriminately. People in tenders should be aware that their craft could be a target of such actions. This behaviour may have a lot to do with partaking of traditional revelries prior to embarking downstream. In 2002 the Yacht Club Regatta is from 28th July to 2nd August, and the Town Regatta from 4th to 10th August. The more sedate Salcombe Festival takes place in June.

The anchorages off Sunny Cove and Smalls Cove on the Portlemouth side are popular in settled weather. Above the ferry on the Salcombe side, the channel into Batson Creek is marked with red/white and green/white poles. This creek leads to the slipway for trailable boats flanked by shallow pontoons, lined with local boats. It stretches northwest from the Normandy short stay pontoon lying off Whitestrand Quay, on which fresh water is available. The quay is the centre of much of the activity and many holiday makers will be found just taking in the scene.

Continuing up the harbour to the northeast, the fuel barge will be ahead and the drying Southpool Lake seen to starboard. Yeowards Boatyard has fore and aft moorings here as well as tidal

Batson Creek Slipway

On the Leading Line

Salcombe Estuary, National Trust, M Rew

moorings further in. At low tide this area of water shrinks to belie the title of 'lake'. Once past the barge The Bag opens up to the north. It is no longer the traditional place to drop the hook as it is now covered in moorings. The visitors' pontoons have helped but the 'knitting' has increased. It may be possible to anchor just north of Snape Point but not in craft of any size. One danger is Mabel Shoal with a depth of a little over one metre at LW Fortunately, the Island Cruising Club headquarters in *Egremont* to the east of it gives a good welcome to visitors.

Visitors passing through this stretch should keep close to the moorings on the east side to just past Haliwell Point if intending to anchor, or pick up a mooring. Many larger craft will find it more appropriate to head for the Pool off Halliwel Point, where there are substantial moorings. An anchorage between Heath Point and Salt Stone just past the landing pontoons, off Linacombe Boatyard, is shown in the information given to visitors, once they have arrived. Most charts show the anchorage nearer Halliwel Point. This a great place from which to explore the creeks that surround this place with an ocean of mud at low water. Timing the tide for such sorties is essential.

From this point, craft will need to make use of the rising tide to proceed to Kingsbridge. From the red buoy off Gurston and Charleton Points the channel is poled and it meanders. Pay strict attention to the poles as you head towards High House Point before moving over to the western side and thence to the Town Quay. Visitors can berth at the visitors' pontoon or alongside the wall. This is past the New Quay. The soft mud berths are accessible about 2 hours either side of High Water Salcombe. Owners of craft intending to travel up to Kingsbridge should seek advice from the helpful harbour staff, especially with regard to mooring and drying out. The maximum length of stay for visitors is one month.

Facilities

There is drinking water available on the Normandy short-stay pontoon off Whitestrand Quay. This pontoon has only one metre of depth at LWS so care may be needed. Maximum length of stay is half an hour. Larger vessels needing water may ask the harbour staff. They can arrange alongside private service, but this will involve a fee. Dinghies may be left on the shoreward side of the pontoon, provided they are clearly marked t/t (name of the parent vessel). There is a floating pontoon at the entrance to Batson Creek on which there is a refuse skip. There are rudimentary public toilets at Creek Car Park and one on Whitestrand Quay. The only showers available to yachtsmen are at the Salcombe Yacht Club or the Island Cruising Club. Local opposition to the building of further public facilities is well known and there is a feeling that it may impinge upon the town. This was touched upon in an article in the *Kingsbridge & Salcombe Gazette*, October 2001. Concern about the decrease in the number of yachts visiting Salcombe was expressed and was followed by correspondence to the editor that may have some impact at a later date.

The services advertised in this section can provide for all contingencies. All telephone numbers are 01548- unless stated. Yeowards Boatyard has full boatyard services including moorings. Telephone –844261 in advance to ensure a place and for further details. For all marine engine, propulsion and electrical problems, Starey Marine should be contacted on 843655. They are able to slip craft up to 30 tonnes. The company runs a 24-hour breakdown service. Danby Maritime Safety is the 'South West Specialist for Marine Safety'. Telephone 842777 for RIBs and inflatables boats, including repairs, as well as all your safety equipment. Call at Watkin Boat Sales, telephone 843383 for *Mariner*, *Quicksilver*, and *Bombard*. They can supply a *Salcombe Flyer* as well as all your surfing requirements for on and off the water. Moorings, outboard repairs and storage are also available.

There are a few shops with a good selection of provisions used to catering for holidaymakers that swell the town in the season. For those who are on holiday from the kitchen, or just do not feel like cooking there is choice. One of the author's favourite places is The Salcombe Coffee Company' in Fore Street, not least because it does superb breakfasts. There are always daily specials on the board for times later in the day. Every one should try their *paninis*. These Italian styled toasted sandwiches are serves with local handmade Burts Crisps. As well as serving the best coffee in town you can get most other beverages and cold drinks. The bar is open for guests and a supper menu is served during July and August. You can take some coffee home in 250g bags as beans or ground.

Salcombe Yacht Club
Cliff Road
Salcombe Devon TQ8 8JG
Tel: 01548-842593 (administration)
01548-842872 (members)

The well-appointed club has many facilities. The club offers toilets, hot showers (coin operated), lounge and patio overlooking the harbour. The bar and restaurant, in the season, offer good food, wine and real beers at sensible prices. Down at the water's edge there is a running mooring to tidal steps next to the club's race start box. Yachtsmen may leave their tenders here whilst they relax in the club. All visiting yachtsmen are welcome and temporary membership is available.

Island Cruising Club
Ferry *Egremont*
Salcombe
Contact telephone number 01548-531775
Visiting yachtsmen are invited aboard the floating club that is situated in the Bag. With showers, a bar (April to October) and occasional bistro, the club attracts many visitors during the year.

View from Salcombe Y C

Close Sailing

Salcombe

Snapes Point, National Trust, M Rew

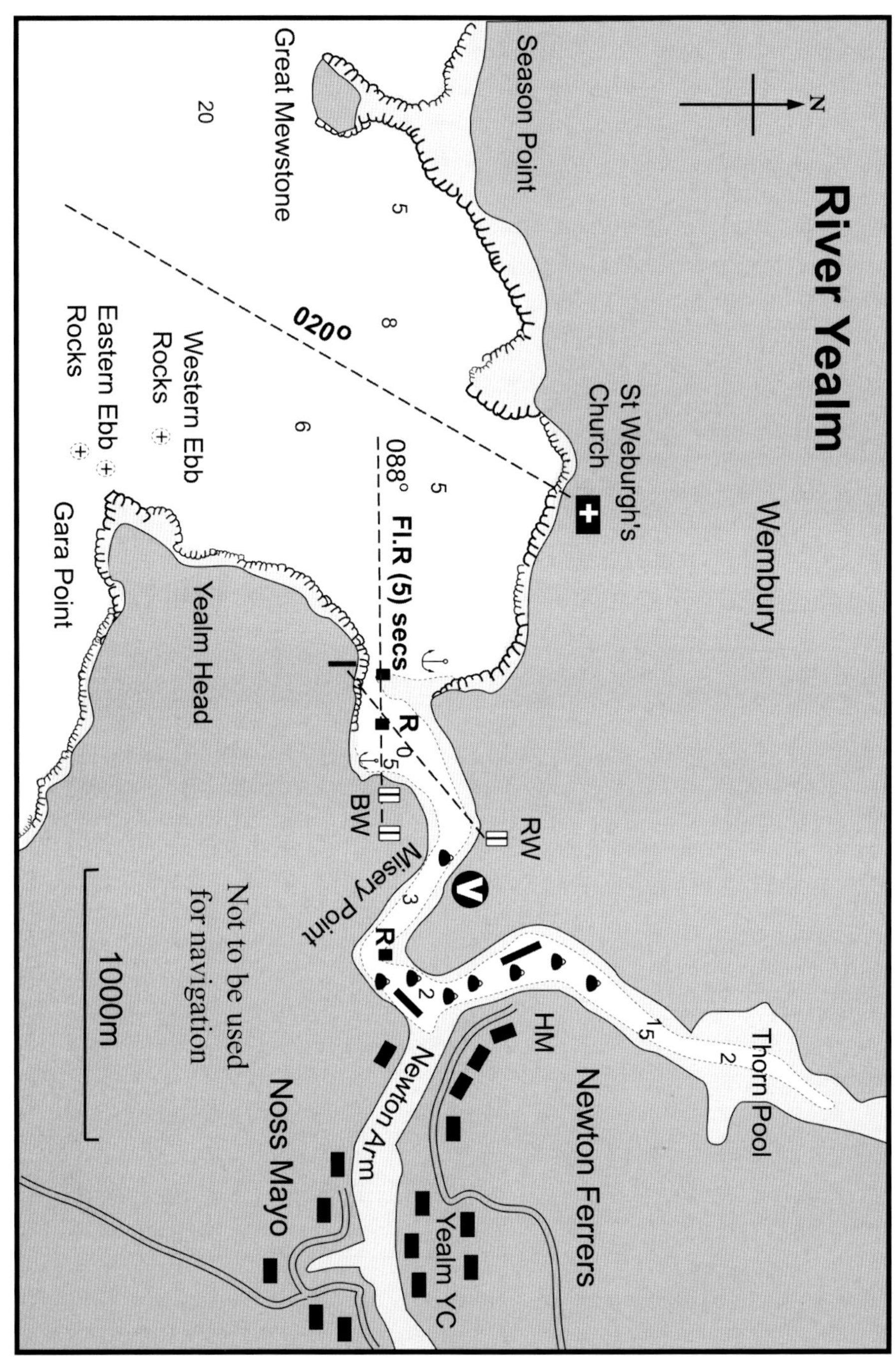
River Yealm
N
Wembury
St Weburgh's Church
Season Point
Great Mewstone
20
5
8
6
5
020°
088°
Fl.R (5) secs
Western Ebb Rocks
Eastern Ebb Rocks
Gara Point
Yealm Head
R
RW
BW
Misery Point
3
2
1.5
2
Thorn Pool
HM
Newton Ferrers
Newton Arm
Yealm YC
Noss Mayo
Not to be used for navigation
1000m

The River Yealm

Charts: Stanfords 13 (Inset) 23, Imray C14, UKHO 30

This largely unspoiled stopover is close to Salcombe. Unfortunately, many people avoid the river in settled weather and Bank Holidays because of the limited mooring space. Speaking to the Harbour Master, I was assured that all craft would be accommodated and the reported restrictions on visiting craft in some pilot books was not correct.

Once in, the shelter is good. The under-developed steep shores of the river means motoring rather than sailing is the order of the day. It should be noted that gusts of wind can accelerate as the steep banks produce a funneling effect. Similarly, the natural bar has contributed to restricting entry. The town of Newton Ferrers reflects the dormitory nature of the area, especially with an increase in the number of holiday homes and the consequential loss of the village-born population.

Road access to the town is limited and bypassed by most traffic. It has not developed tourism like some of the showier towns along the South Coast. Fortunately, it does not attract many who are looking for more action. The National Trust has acquired much of the coastline and land around Noss Mayo and on the Wembury side of the estuary. The coastal path may be walked from Netton to Gara Head. The South Devon Coast Path follows the river right out to Yealm Head. A good map is essential for walkers who wish to explore this spectacular stretch of coastline. OS Pathfinder 1362 is recommended in the River Yealm Harbour guide. It lists details of seven walks for the country-lover. As most of the landing on the banks of the Yealm are private, it is mainly though the efforts of the National Trust that so much of the area can be walked.

The name Newton Ferrers comes from Henri de Ferrieres. He was a Norman knight given the lands around this area by William I. It was his payment for taking part in the conquest of England. It is listed in the Doomsday Book (1086) as the 'New Town'. The old town was Yealmton. The village was 'developed' in the early twentieth century and has remained largely unspoiled until today.

River Yealm

Bolt Head from Gara Rock, National Trust, M Rew

Approach

Coming from the west, round the Great Mew Stone and clear the shallow Mewstone Ledge almost half a mile to the southwest. Once well clear, continue eastward until past the shoreward Outer Slimmer to head north of east and aim to pass Mouthstone ledge to the northwest of Yealm Head. Craft should clear Mouthstone Ledge by about half a mile to pick up the leading marks onshore in Cellar Bay. These will come into line when they bear just north of east. Craft will be well into the bay before the entrance opens up.

From the east, the unlit Yealm Head needs to be given an offing of half a mile. The Eastern and Western Ebb Rocks should be avoided. Both rocks can be awash at low water springs (LWS). Stay south of 50°18′N until the 44 m high tower of St. Wembury Church shows east of North. Slowly turn into the bay whilst ensuring the tower bears more than 010°. See sketch map.

The Sand Bar stretches across the entrance leaving a navigable gap of only 40 metres. The approach is assisted by the two white triangular marks with black central stripes on a bearing of 088°. North of this line will avoid the Mouthstone Ledge, off the point of the same name. During the last few years the bar has grown and a second red buoy (unlit) has been laid to assist passage. One should not attempt to cross the river towards the square white marker with a central vertical red stripe until the outer Fl.R. 5 sec. and the inner unlit buoys have been left to port on entry. Do not cut the corner, as the Cellar Bay line does not clear the edge of the bar. To avoid any uncertainty, it will be prudent to wait until a couple of hours after LW.

Once in, leaving the green beacon to starboard and the second red buoy to port, the mark on the north shore, a white board with a red stripe, should be identified. Head for it on a course of about 050°. Care should be taken as the Bar reaches up to the second red buoy. A few small craft use the daytime anchorage in Cellar Bay during settled weather. The depth of water will increase as you head for the mark. Once past the wooded Misery Point there should be plenty of water in the channel up to Madge Point and the scrubbing posts. Above these there are oyster beds. Anchoring is prohibited over these and is restrictive elsewhere. Yachts need the Harbour Master's permission to anchor. One pilot book suggests that the level of charging is arbitrary and subject to the season, but this is not so. There is a discount for visits over 5 days duration.

Visitors are not allowed to anchor up-river of Madge Point. The oyster beds stretch past the beacons marking the electric cables running below the mud and Court Wood. Beyond this there are moorings, several drying, centred around Thorn Pool. This area opposite Shallowford Creek has depths of over 2 metres.

Harbour Master

River Yealm River Authority
Harbour Office
Yealm Hotel Drive
Newton Ferrers
Devon PL8 1BL

There is a visitors' mooring that will take large craft (up to 25 metres) just east of Misery Point and the line of private moorings will lead you into the Pool. Do not disregard The Spit buoy as it marks the inside edge of the bend. There are three 25 ton moorings in the southern part that will take up to three boats. Continuing around the bend the 45 metre long pontoon will be seen. The moorings

Looking towards Yealm Entrance, National Trust, R Hillgrove

run past the quay and floating pontoon. From here, the river runs north past the town and the Newtown Ferrers Arm to starboard that dries out.

Hidden by the greenery is the harbour master's office that can be found in Hotel Drive leading to the conspicuous Yealm Hotel. Take the steps up to the road in front of the hotel. There appears to be no VHF watch. Dinghies left at the Yealm Steps pontoon must not obstruct the deep-water side. Craft can berth up to half an hour to take on water or dispose of bagged rubbish. The bins are nearby. Further up the river on the western side is another visitors' pontoon. Fortunately, the harbour staff usually meets and advises most visiting craft. If you do not meet up with them, you can call at the office if you have a query.

Newton Ferrers

During the season the town activity increases but at a sedate pace. Here, you will find the tempo breaks into a brisk walk when the visitors' dinghies head for the shore in the evening. Timing the tide, one can travel by dinghy to the Yealm Yacht Club on the north side of Newton Creek, just past the causeway. The club welcomes visitors and has showers for the use of visiting yachtsmen. The continental-style restaurant (in the season) is a great excuse for the galley team to do some research. See *Some Local Clubs* for more information. The attraction of the Yealm is that you can get away from it all. Even mobile phones get a holiday!

Yealm YC

Plymouth

Charts Stanfords 13, 22 Imray C14, UKHO SC5602

From Drake to Dreadnought, the city has been the centre of Naval History and tradition. Sadly, the reduction of the size of the Royal Navy and the decline in Plymouth's fortunes are inter-twined. Names like Cabot and Cockerham, Hawkins and Gilbert spring to mind. Exploration and sorties against the French, and trade across the Atlantic following the steps of the Pilgrim Fathers, all helped to make this England's foremost port for many years. It was very fitting that the "other Sir Francis", Chichester, made Plymouth his port for the successful circumnavigation in 1966/7.

During the Second World War, the city and the Royal Dockyard of Devonport were targeted and sustained great damage. Since then, much has been re-built. The information technology age has helped to make the city a new centre of activity and there are plans to expand the city's role in this essential modern industry. Whatever has happened, Plymouth has been tied to the sea and the lives of seafarers. Today, the Fleet still sails into Devonport- in ones and twos- in competition with the increasing number of modern leisure craft filling the space created by the decline in dock work. The ferries to France and Spain, the fishing fleet and commercial fishing make this a busy port. Yachtsmen will know the port as the start of the short-handed Transatlantic races and the end of the biennial Fastnet Race. As a superb natural harbour, very few ports can rival Plymouth.

The ferries use Milbay Docks and the Queen's Harbour Master, VHF 16/14, call sign Longroom Port Control, controls movements in tidal waters, telephone 01752-836952. Traffic signal lights are displayed from a mast on Drake's Island and relayed from Flagstaff at Devonport for vessels in the Hamoaze. When they are displayed all craft should call to ask permission to cross. Restrictions of movements are displayed. For Signals see below.

Plymouth Harbour Traffic Signals

1 occulting red light over 2 occulting greens	outgoing traffic only
2 occulting green lights over 1 occulting red	incoming traffic only
2 occulting green lights over 1 occulting white	vessels can proceed in each direction
3 vertical flashing red lights	Give a wide berth to naval vessels
	All traffic suspended
	Movements directed solely by QHM
No lights exhibited	All vessels can proceed

Vessels are reminded that IRPCS Rule 9 applies at all times.

There is a wind warning that can be displayed when there is no traffic signal shown.

1 occulting white light Wind force 5-7 2 occulting white lights Wind over force 7

These are re-enforced by wind flags at marinas.

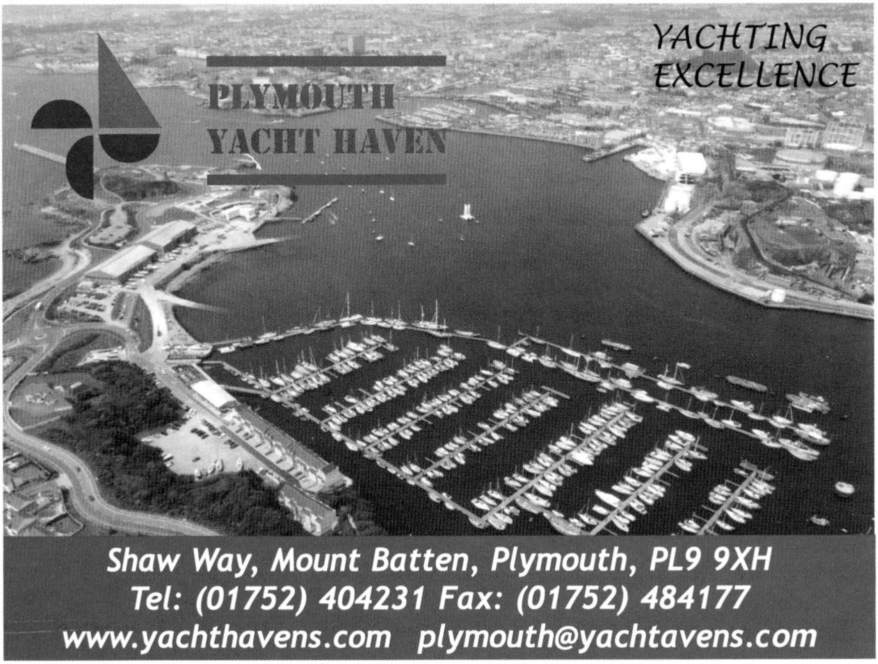

Plymouth Sound, Bridgend Boat Company

Reproduced from Stanfords Chart 13, by kind permission of Stanfords Charts, the Controller of Her Majesty's Stationery Office and the UK Hydrographic Office

The Plymouth area has attractions for those who enjoy the outdoors. Walkers will find an excellent route taking them along the Plymouth Waterfront Walk. For those who prefer the open spaces and the views of the Sound, The regular ferry links the Barbican and Mount Batten. On the south side you can pick up the South Devon Coastal Path. A route which take you along the coast towards Bovisan Fort and returning leisurely. At the Mount Batten Centre, on your return, you can take refreshment overlooking the moorings and keep watch for the ferry.

The more ambitious could hire a cycle from Plymouth Cycle Hire in Queen Anne's Battery, where there are free showers for hire customers and safe car parking. From here the South West Coast Path can be followed northward to

Saltram House and the park maintained by the National Trust. Here, the cycle trail skirts the Plym estuary which attracts a multitude of wading birds, Oystercatchers, Curlew and Egrets. The trail continues along the Great Western railway that winds through the beautiful Plym Valley, criss-crossing it on towering Brunel viaducts overlooking the woodland canopy, towards Dartmoor. There are some ideal places for a picnic.

Drake's Island in the fog

If you are feeling really energetic, follow the trail to Clearbrook, where you can visit the Skylark pub for a drink and some lunch. For more information Contact Plymouth Cycle Hire on 01752-258944.

Approach

From the west, anchoring in Cawsand Bay is an option in winds from the westerly quadrant. The bottom shelves gradually and the holding is good although it can get a little crowded in periods of settled weather. Continuing past the breakwater the red buoys mark the deep-water channel past Drake Island. North of Melampus Buoy, Fl.R. 4 sec. light, will be seen the Winter bank marked by cardinal buoys on the east (starboard) side of Asia Pass. The Fl.R.(2) 5 sec. red buoy indicates the port side off Drake's Island. Craft can head for the Hamoaze, Tamar or the private Mill Bay Village Marina seen ahead. Note traffic signals mentioned earlier.

Cycle Trail, D Edwards

Plymouth Sound lies between Great Mew Stone off Wembury Rock to the west and Penlee Point to the east. See 'Looe to Plymouth' for approach to the Plymouth Breakwater from the west. Apart from Tinker, a shoal patch with depths less than 4 metres, marked by a west and an east cardinal buoy there are no dangers for small craft approaching the sectored L.Fl.W.R. 10 sec. light, range 8/6 miles on the west end of the

Classic Boats, B Blackler, PYH

Breakwater. Craft will leave the Shag Stone beacon well to starboard.

In easterly winds you may wish to anchor in Jennycliff Bay inshore and south of the Fl.G. 6 sec. wreck buoy and northward of the sectored Withyhedge Light in about 4 metres. To the north of the bay is the water-ski area.

Once past, there is no danger for craft heading for Plymouth Yacht Haven, Queen Anne's Battery and Sutton Marina, see later. Yachts need not keep to the deep-water channel, before rounding the Fl.G (3) 10 sec. light on the restored Mount Batten pier. The Mount Batten Centre is situated just past the ferry terminal. The regular timetabled service is a great way to visit the Barbican and the centre of Plymouth. Backing the peninsula are the large hangers housing Western Marine Power, Bridgend Boat Company and Rock Run Yachts. You will have the choice of havens in the Cattewater.

The Cattewater

This is administered separately by the Cattewater Harbour Commissioners, telephone 01752-665934. Once north of the Mount Batten pier the Plymouth Yacht Haven comes into view on the Turnchapel side. Beyond it is the lit channel leading up

Cattewater and Laira Bridge

the River Plym to Plym Yacht Club. Before reaching the PYC, the dinghy rack situated on the starboard side of the entrance to Hooe Lake will identify the The Hooe Lake Yacht Club. Craft of 30 foot or under visiting the PYC may be able to find a temporary mooring. It may be sensible to telephone the club in advance to inquire, see *Local Clubs*. Beyond these are two boatyards where craft can be laid up. On the port hand side before the Laira Bridge is Shore Store, where there are lay up facilities, pontoon moorings and chandlery. To port from here is Rocky Pindar Boatyard. Craft are laid up on Pomphlett Quay over-looking the tranquil half-tide moorings. Both have easy road access and are well served by public transport.

When heading for Hamoaze and the Tamar continue to round the island to port and then Devil's Point to starboard. Shallow draft craft can take a short cut leaving the island to starboard. The Bridge with at least 2 metres depth can be identified using the lit beacons. The quick green and quick red ones are at the south-west entrance with the Fl.G.(3) 10sec. and Fl.R.(4) 10 sec. at the north-west. Approaching the pass on a course of 333° the edge of Devil's Point is in line with conspicuous house that has three chimneys on the Devonport shore. Many local craft use this entry, which is the shorter route in good conditions. The course keeps craft off some underwater obstructions to the south and it is recommended that vessels continue until north of the red beacon.

To port and ahead is Barn Pool. The northern part has long been recognized as a yacht anchorage, but you should buoy your anchor. Tucked in to the wooded shore you will be out of the tide, and although there are some eddies their effect is slight. One can land at the beach to follow the coastal path through Edgcumbe Park towards Cawsand, or northward to Cremyll to the Edgcumbe Arms. It is only a short trip by motorized dinghy to the pub and landing is on the beach next to the ferry slip. Do not obstruct the slip.

By now, Mayflower International Marina will come into view to starboard in front of the distinctive Ocean Court Flats. A winner of the '*Five Gold Anchor'* award, a consortium of berth holders owns this marine development. It has shown how successful the integration of residential and marine leisure usage can work.

Plymouth Marinas (in alphabetical order)

Mayflower International Marina

Ocean Quay, Richmond Walk
Plymouth PL1 4LS
Tel: 01752-556633
Email:
mayflower@mayflowermarina.co.uk

For many yachtsmen, Mayflower International Marina is synonymous with yachting in Plymouth. Conveniently placed at the beginning of the Tamar River, it commands superb views of the Cornish side of the estuary. From here, the magnificent grounds of Mount Edgcumbe House give a relaxed and calming ambiance. It is first choice for many visitors to the area. The courtesy bus to and from the city centre during July and August makes it convenient for changing crew or leaving your yacht and getting to the main line train station. As a member of Transmanche Marinas it maintains the highest international standards

As you approach call *Mayflower Marina* on VHF Ch 80/37 and you will probably be allocated a berth. If you need assistance manoeuvering someone will be there to meet you. The marina office is manned 0800 – 1800 daily, as well as 24 hour security outside office hours when you should tie up to the reception berth, marked by flags, on the outside pontoon. The directional light for nighttime approach will assist, as will the two vertical fixed lights on the outer pontoons.

As a Transmanche Marina all facilities are available, the ample berths have water and electricity, whilst shoreside there are toilets and showers, bar and restaurant. Services range from 25 ton boat hoist to a complete fuel service, diesel, petrol, LPG, paraffin, 2-stroke oils, calor/camping gas. Also available are all marine and rigging services. On Richmond Walk you will find Eurospars, for all your rigging needs, and

Ösen Sails for new sails and covers, as well as repairs.

The staff at the marina office, that overlooks the berths, can help with most inquires and local information. There is a weather/tourist booth below the office for visitors and berth holders where full weather forecasts and tourist brochures can be found.

Plymouth Yacht Haven Ltd
Shaw Way, Mount Batten
Plymouth PL9 9XH
Tel: 01752-404231
Fax: 01752-484177
Homepage: www.yachthavens.com
Email: plymhaven@aol.com
Located in Clovelly Bay at the mouth of the Cattewater, the marina is sheltered from the prevailing southwesterly winds. The 450 berths cater for vessels up to 45m in length and 7m draft, so all visitors will be able to find a suitable berth, alongside or on a finger. Within easy reach of the marina are superb coastal walks, a golf course, gym and fitness center. The Mount Batten Centre where visitors can relax with a drink, or two, is only a short walk away. Alternatively, a stroll to Turnchapel to one of the pubs/restaurants will make a pleasant evening. There is a regular bus service, Poute 7, into Plymstock and Plymouth.

Approaching Plymouth Yacht Haven call VHF Ch 37/80 for advice on berthing. There is always a member of staff available to help. With a long-keeled yacht

Plymouth Yacht Haven, B Blackler

that does not turn on a sixpence, a helping hand on arrival is a must and this can be requested over the radio. If you need diesel, or berthing inside the outer pontoon, the entrance is clearly marked at the eastern end of the marina. There is plenty of space for passage between pontoon P1 and the finger berths. This is a convenient place to leave your boat, if you are called away. The ferry from Mount Batten puts you in the Barbican in minutes, or you can take the bus service to the coach or rail station. If you need a taxi, there is a freephone service from reception.

A full range of facilities and services is offered on site, hot showers, toilets, laundrette (tokens from the office), 24 hour security (contact on VHF 37/80 or 07721 498422 out of office hours) and weather information. At reception there is an Email service for visitors, photocopying and fax, and the staff can supply ice. There are payphones for berth holders' use.

Marine services include a 65 tonne boat hoist and ample hard standing, electrical and electronic engineers, boat repairers and riggers, a sail collection point, and a washing, scrubbing and antifouling service. Westways have yachts for charter, sale and on brokerage. The well-stocked Mount Batten Chandlery and R C Tremblett (Upholsterers) will be able to supply equipment for above and below decks. Two companies housed in the Mount Batten Hangers are Western Marine Power Ltd, marine electrical and mechanical experts, and Bridgend Boat Company Ltd, highly skilled repairers and builders of traditional and modern craft. Both have excellent facilities and plenty of hard standing.

Queen Anne's Battery Marina

Plymouth
Devon PL4 0LP
Tel: 01752-671142

Queen Anne's Battery Marina, on the opposite side of the lock to The Barbican, is owned by MDL. It is on the site of the gun emplacements built during the Napoleonic Wars. Call VHF Ch 80 on approach during office hours. There are 250 berths for boats up to 18m LOA. Visitors will probably have to raft up on the outside pontoon, just inside the breakwater, in the season. The finishers of the Fastnet Race in 2001 rafted up to swap stories, wait for the provisional results and relax. The marina has all of the usual facilities on the finger berths. The office is upstairs in the building nearest the water next, to the ANCASTA offices. On shore, there are showers, toilets and places to eat, including the Royal Western YC restaurant silver service (open daily). There are many excellent services operating on the site, please consult the *List of Advertisers* to find advertisements not listed in this section. There is a 20-ton slipway boat hoist and ample hard standing.

Since the club moved here in 1988, the Royal Western Yacht Club of England has overlooked the marina. It is open 0900 – 2300, in the season, and welcomes visiting bona-fide yachtsmen. In the same building is Sea Chest, Admiralty Chart Agents well known for their new and secondhand nautical books. The latest venture is nautical jigsaws based on charts, just the thing for a Christmas present.

If you need anything electrical or electronic, why not pop in and see the specialists, Waypoint 1; their office is next to *RYA*-recognised Plymouth Sailing School. If you need to be better qualified then this should be your port of call. The following services are available, yacht repairers Fast Tack Yachts, Inshore Covers for all your covers and sail repairs, David Edwards Marine Services, Plymouth Cycle Hire, and Allspars. Also, within the complex is the Yacht Parts Plymouth chandlery. At the entrance you will find

Eurospars, as well as Phoenix 316, stainless steel fabricators.

Nearby, in Commercial Road are fabricators Aqua-tech Marine, Stainless Steel Centre for fastenings and Yacht Rigging Services. A few blocks away, in Alvington Street, is Marco Marine, the Yanmar specialists, with a range of quality marine products.

Sutton Yacht Harbour Marina

Sutton Harbour Company
North Quay House
Sutton Harbour
Plymouth PL4 0RA
Tel: 01752-204168

Situated adjacent to The Barbican, this harbour has a long history going back to the days of Elizabeth 1. It has a lock to maintain depth that can be crossed by a swing footbridge. Call *Sutton Harbour Radio* on VHF CH 80 (24 hours). There are lights, green for go, red for stop and flashing red could mean a long wait. Once the lock is opened, the harbour office is directly ahead on entry overlooking the fuel berth. The visitor berths are on the pontoons to the right of this. On the west side of the dock wall at the pedestrian walkway exit, is the Barbican Yacht Agency and further along the quayside is the only chandlery shop in the Barbican, Marine Bazaar. The ablution block is further along the quay at the corner of the dock. Sutton Harbour is the home of the Plymouth fishing fleet and most services are available.

Hamoaze

Back in the main river as you head north through the Narrows, Mount Edgcumbe slips by. The view opens up to show St. John's Lake and Millbrook to port. The area of water at high water becomes a shiny expanse of mud at low water opposite H.M. Devonport Naval Base. The latter "lake" leads to Southdown Marina. It has tidal access- HW +/- 3 hours. Craft should keep the right hand tower (of three) and the large blue shed in line astern until a pink house to port appears abeam. Then head for the first gap in the pontoons to starboard. You may telephone ahead to be met during your approach on 01752-823084.

The Torpoint/Devonport chain ferry will be seen before the Royal Dockyard on the Devonside. HMS Drake , the naval base, is all that is left of one of the biggest military establishments in Europe. The Devonport Royal Dockyard is now a private company that has been involved in some high profile contracts, including the new generation of lifeboats.

Of more interest to the yachtsman is the Torpoint Yacht Harbour opposite. The history of the Ballast Yard is reflected in the walls, some 6 metres thick. It is dredged to 2 metres. The half tide access to the 80 pontoon berths enables visitors to enter although it is extremely tight. There are very few berths that can be used for short stays, though you will need to telephone ahead to ensure a berth, 01752-813658. Water and electricity are available, showers and toilets are on shore. The friendly Torpoint Tornado Sailing Club is well worth a visit, when it is open. See clubs information later. Once past the chain ferries and the deep water ship basins to starboard the bridges ahead will be seen over the land. On the bend in the Tamar the River Lynher will open up to port. During the life of this book, one should see the building of a naval loading jetty on the Devon side against which warships will berth. It will probably involve restrictions on leisure craft whilst there are ship movements.

River Lynher

The Lynher River (St Germans River) is navigable up to St. Germans Quay. It may be possible to lie alongside the quay, by arrangement. Bilge-keelers can dry out here. Leave the Lynher Buoy, Q.R., to the south to head up the channel leaving the moorings off Wearde Quay to starboard. There is room to anchor just past the moorings in Sand Acre Bay, and it is possible to land by dinghy. One should keep Beggars Island red buoys to port and not cut the next corner, marked by G.Fl. buoy, before the channel crosses to the north shore off Anthony Passage, where a red buoy indicates the port hand of the channel. One can anchor here and row ashore. On the opposite bank is the Royal Navy School of Seamanship, off Jupiter Point.

There are electric cables and a pipeline with attendant bankside beacons in the next reach of the river that sweeps round past Ince Point. The Ince green buoy off Black Rock may be passed closely.

Shallow draft boats could anchor off Ince Quay during neaps, but remember the tide is about 0.5 m less than at Plymouth. This is not so noticeable in fresh southerlies and during low pressure. The channel heads towards the red buoy before it gently curves towards the Dandy Hole. With about 3 m depth at low water this isolated spot has become a local favourite anchorage, so you may not be alone. Fortunately, with no shoreside development, it attracts like minds.

Red and green poles indicate the channel for the last drying leg to the quay. You may ask at the club if you need to find a berth or dry out alongside. When the club is closed there is a board with a telephone number for information. A more certain choice would be to telephone the Lynher Boatyard (01503-230132) at the Creekside Quay, Polbathic. Visitors can be met lower down the river by arrangement. This creek is to po… approach St. Germans Quay.

From St. Germans Quay the river branches north towards the viaduct (clearance 20 metres). 'Boating World' is just beyond. There are second-hand boats for sale, chandlery, marine engineers and a 10 ton crane. It is only a quick trip in the dinghy if you are visiting the club.

Upper Reaches of River Tamar

North of the Lynher River the Tamar runs under both the Brunel railway bridge and the road bridge built in 1961. Both have air space of 30 m or more. South of them are trots of moorings flanking of the channel. On the west bank and dwarfed by the structures linking Cornwall and Devon is Saltash. Only the large slipway reminds us of the Tamar Ferry that fell victim to the building of the second bridge.

Saltash

Weir Quay, M Hooton

That, and the number of pubs are modern reminders of the prosperity when Saltash was on the main thoroughfare to Cornwall.

The Saltash Sailing Club is open most days at lunchtime and in the evenings. The short stay pontoon has water except at low water spring when care is needed. If you intend to visit the club or one of the local hostelries then berth temporarily to establish if a club mooring can be allocated for your stay. The ebb is strong, up to 5 knots so the locals say, so anchoring, even on a long scope, is not an option. Certainly, for craft up to 30 feet there are possible short stay moorings. One should be aware

Sketch Drawing of the Upper Reaches of the Tamar

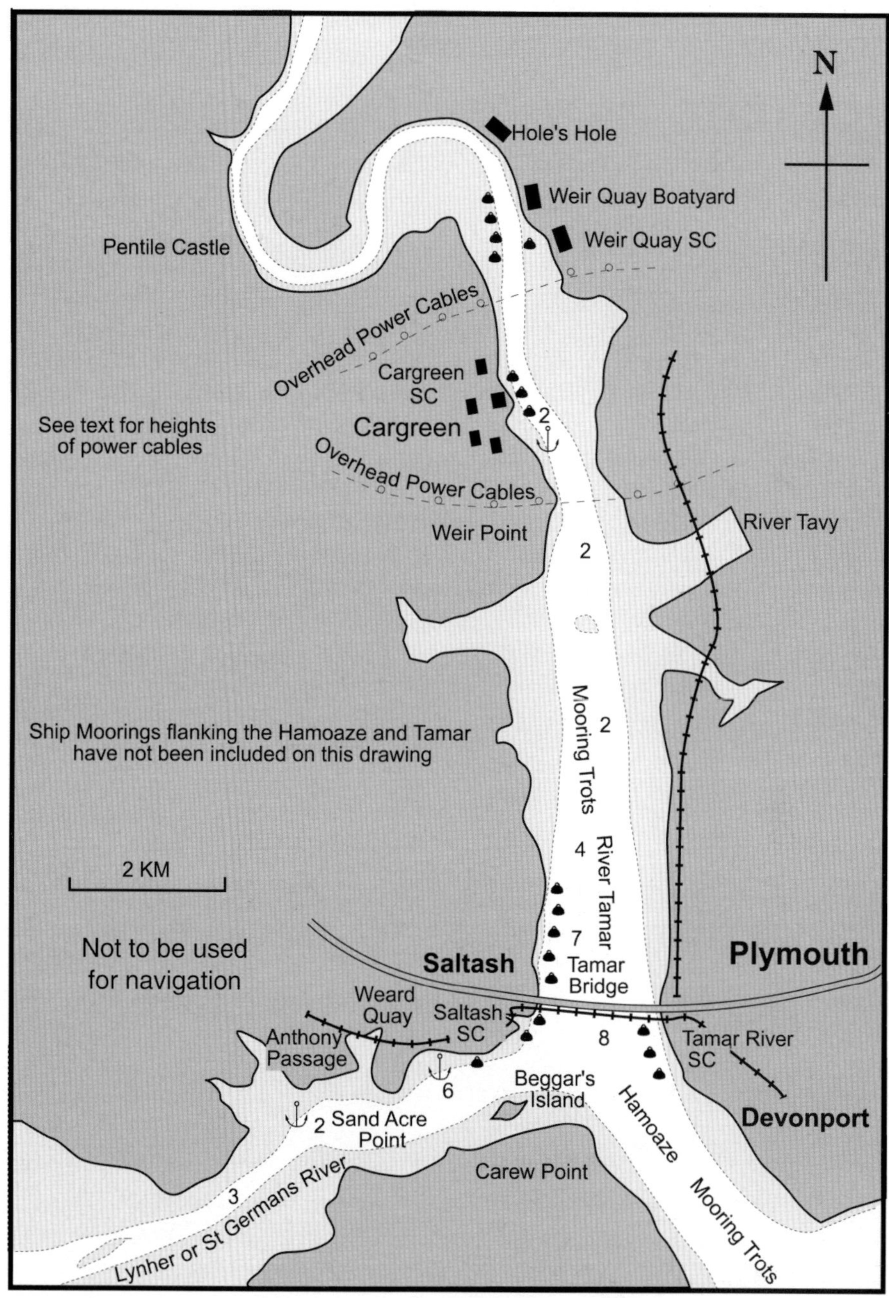

One should be aware that the buoys are roped together in trots. A greater danger is the floating debris that can increase after periods of heavy rain. On the eastern shore is the friendly Tamar River Sailing Club with its refurbished clubhouse and 23 m floating pontoon. There is water at all states of tide and a hoist to help the disabled. They can often find a mooring for visitors. Just go alongside and ask at the club.

Craft used to anchor opposite the entrance to Saltmill Creek just north of the bridges, on the edge of the fairway, but it is a long row by dinghy to shore. There is a 'hole' with about 4 metres plus LAT. Nowadays; many cruising craft go no further as the overhead power cables between Weir Point and Lime Point put them off. However, the air space is about 20 m. Those craft that have continued northward will keep the four green buoys close to starboard and aim to pass midway between the yellow buoy and Weir Point. Be guided by the moorings as the river bends to the northwest past Cargreen where landing is easy.

One may be able to pick up a visitor mooring owned by the Crooked Spaniard's Inn. Alternatively, one could anchor outside the moorings and go ashore to enjoy some good food. The modern Cargreen Yacht Club partly funded with lottery money is open in the season. It is further along on the port side. Visitors are welcome. The club has a bar and showers that could make a stop worthwhile. The best time is weekends and Friday night in the season

From Cargreen the channel heads north with less depth. Apart from the green beacon marking the 'lump' off Thorn Point, where the channel narrows, there are no more marks. Craft should aim to pass the moorings and the slip at Weir

Moorings at Weir Quay, M Hooton

Quay Boatyard on the starboard side, closely. Just before the Weir Quay Sailing Club (see *Local Clubs*) and the boatyard are power lines stretching across the river. The restriction in height varies according to the sources checked. The lowest figure given, 16 m at HWS, is enough to deter many sailing craft. However, from observation there are certainly boats with much greater airspace than that berthed at the yard and on the moorings. One such boat was a 50-foot ex-Canada Cup yacht and there were several of over 40 foot in January 2002. At the wires, the channel tends to the east of the centre of the wire span and that will give, at least, another couple of metres at HWS. Working the tide will give another couple of metres clearance, i.e. about 20 m. You can always telephone Weir Quay boatyard for information, 01822-840474.

The yard has a shop for most immediate provisions, chandlery, gas, fuels and water. The boat transporter can handle up to 14 tons and there are moorings for visitors off the quay. With at least 2 metres depth over soft mud one can lie comfortably in what is arguably the most superb setting on the Tamar. Train buffs will know the Tamar Valley Line runs through Bere Alston and Bere Ferrers, making a perfect excursion along the picturesque valley to Plymouth.

After Weir Quay comes Hole's Hole and the Clifton Bend leading to South Hooe. Here, the channel is deeper on the outside of the curve, and leads to an ideal spot in a southerly blow before Pentille Castle and the quay of the same name. If you do want to make it further remember there is only a metre and a half of water at high tide so only craft with shallow draft should venture past the southern point of the South Hooe peninsula. The river continues this pattern to Cotehele Quay where the National Trust has a permanent exhibition

Cotehele Quay, National Trust, A Besley

including *Shamrock*, a Tamar barge. The final leg to Calstock is over half a mile.

Cotehele

Craft drawing one metre or less can continue to Cotelele Quay to visit the large estate formally owned by the Edgcumbe family for about 600 years. Today, the National Trust maintains one of the least-altered grand medieval houses and the surrounding parkland. Lying alongside the quay is a short term option but you must keep clear of the ferry berth. Of course, the crews of deeper draught boats can make a trip by dinghy, and it is an opportunity not to be missed. The splendour is complete with original furniture, armour and a fine collection of tapestries. The Great hall, a very fine example of an arch-braced roof, conjures up pictures of Tudor lords and ladies. The chapel dates back to the same time as the house. Although the oldest working clock is from later era, it is still in its original position.

Cotelele is not just a house, it is a wooded fantasy where you can linger during riverside walks to the quay, and Cotehele Mill alongside the Morden stream. The mill still works and water flows seaward from this tranquil setting. Water played a great part in the history of the estate and this is recognised by the well preserved Tamar barge *Shamrock*. This 56 foot ketch, built at the turn of the 19th century was lovingly restored and is jointly owned by the National Trust and the National Maritime Museum. She is moored as if ready to set off on one of her trading runs, and is sometimes sailed by modernday enthusiasts. More importantly, she is almost the last example of the vessels that supplied the needs of the people in more leisurely days.

A day out would not be complete without a souvenir. In Sir Richard Edgcumbe's barn is the National Trust Shop, which sells a wide selection of gifts and plants. The licensed barn restaurant serves a range of home-cooked meals especially suited to dining out in one of England's finest historic estates.

Looe Harbour

Charts. Stanfords Charts 13, Imray C6 (Inset), UKHO BA 147

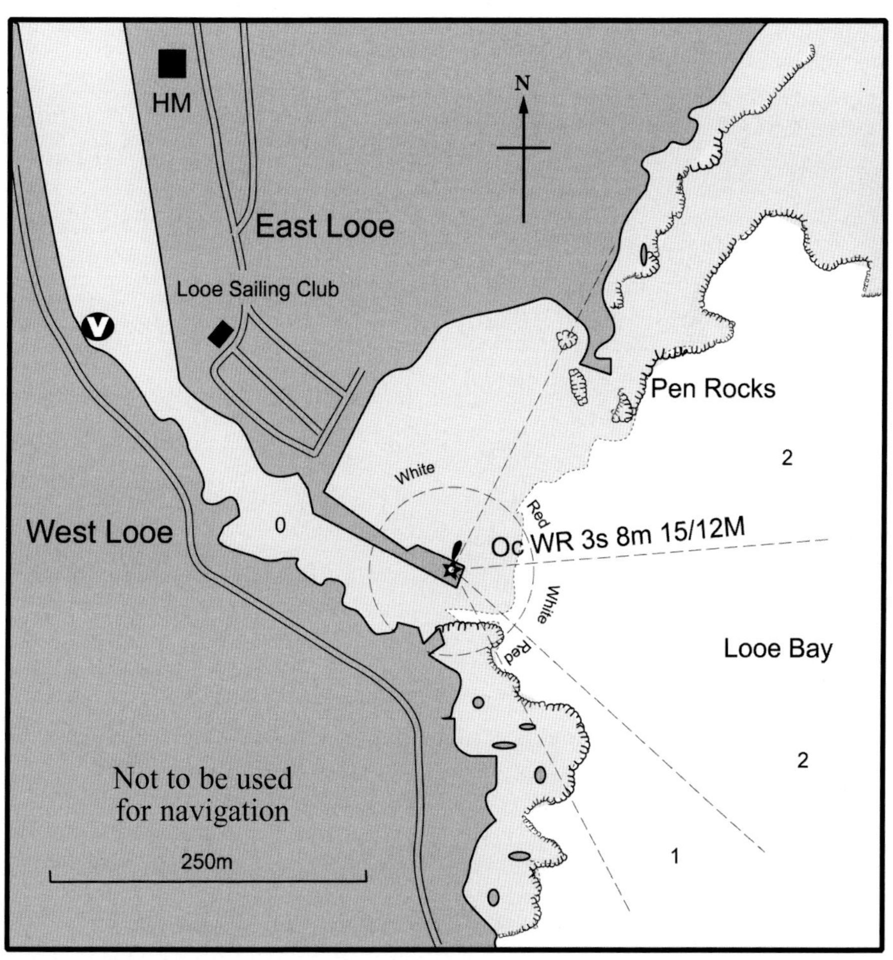

Looe to Plymouth

Craft heading for Plymouth from the West will have choices of where to stop. See Lizard to Looe in the *Afloat & Ashore* series, available in most boating shops or from the authors. From south of Looe Island, yachts can round up to anchor off this traditional fishing village. The Island, (also known as St.Georges Island) was the location for the book *'We Bought an Island'* about two sisters who left the Home Counties for the good country life. In fresh weather craft should continue past and stay below 50°19´N to avoid overfalls. In settled weather with winds from west to north one can wait to enter. Anchor in 3/4 metres of water to the east off the sectored Banjo Pierhead light, Occ. W.R. 3 sec. range 12 miles approximate position 50°21´N 04°27´W. To avoid the force of the tide rushing out advice is to anchor north of a line with the light above bearing 290º, but well away from Pen Rocks to the north.

Visitors may find they can tie up to the visitors' berth on the west side of the harbour. The one visitor's alongside drying berth is marked on the building just past the steps down to the old ferry. A fender board will be a great asset as craft dry out on gravel and sand. The bottom is hard. Do not anchor where there are moorings for local boats and pipelines across the river. If you need assistance or information call the Looe Harbour Master on VHF Channel 16, call sign *Looe Harbour*. Alternatively, you can telephone 01503-262839. The Harbour Office in the fish market on the east quay is open 0900-1800 in the season. Beware of boat movements, not least the self-hire motor boats popular with visitors to this quaint Cornish fishing village. Boats will need sufficient engine power to counteract the swift tidal stream.

Fresh water is available on both quays and there is a small shower/toilet block in the Visitors Berths building. Both diesel and petrol are available on the east quay or in cans. Most services associated with the coastal fishing industry are available. Shopping is geared to the needs of the local population and the tourists who crowd into the town during the season. Shops are open on Sundays during the summer.

Looe Sailing Club near the root of the pier extends a warm welcome to visitors. It has showers and a licensed bar. There is a fair choice of pubs and restaurants to satisfy most tastes. Those who are interested in the heritage of 'Living from the Sea' will be able to see the exhibition in the Guildhall in East Looe. As if not to be outdone, the SE Cornwall Discovery Centre in West Looe is well worth a visit.

From the longitude of Looe, apart from the shoal patch in approximately 50°20´N 04°23´W there are no further dangers before Rame Head. Craft heading for Plymouth Sound will be well south of this.

Rame Head is unlit and as a ruin on its summit. From well offshore its distinctive symmetrical shape is described in many

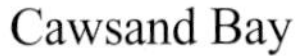

Cawsand Bay

pilot books. At night, the red lights on the radio mast further inshore will show up from the west, backed by the loom of the city. Before turning into the Sound craft need to clear the wooded Penlee Point and the off-lying Draystone Rocks. The Fl.R. (2) 5 sec. buoy in position 50°18.5´N 04°11´W must be left landward on entry. This will bring craft to the edge of the isophase sector of the light on the western end of the Plymouth Breakwater. Craft may wish to anchor in Cawsand Bay to avoid ship movements, commercial and naval, in poor visibility or at night in sttled weather. The bottom shelves gradually and the holding is good. In winds from the western quadrant there is good shelter.

The pilotage must include the ONE offshore feature which has dominated the history of Plymouth. So much so that the city removed the Smeaton Tower from the Eddystone Rocks and re-built it on the famous Hoe. The present lighthouse (Sir J Douglas, 1882) at 41 metres dominates. The Fl.W. (2) 10 sec. light in position 50°10.8´N 04°15.9´W has a range of 20 miles and is re-enforced in poor visibility by a Horn (3) 60 sec. Vessels with radar will make use of the RACON (T) housed in the red lantern house. The red sector light at 28 metres shines over the Hand Deeps. The Fl.Y. 5 sec. buoy marks the northern edge of the bank of less than 10 metres. Any craft crossing the area will be thankful for at least one light visible for most of the passage from the Start to Fowey, or further west.

Western Breakwater, Plymouth

Local Clubs

To be included in subsequent editions club secretaries should contact the editor in writing.

Cargreen Yacht Club
Coombe Lane, Cargreen,
Saltash, Cornwall PL12 6UG
Tel: 01579-350313
Email: john@claptrap.org.uk
Contact the Hon. Secretary on 01579-350313
The club is about 400 metres north of Cargreen village, 2 miles north of the Saltash bridge. The clubhouse was funded by the National Lottery and was built in 1994. The club has a very active dinghy programme. Facilties include a bar, showers and a slipway.

Island Cruising Club
Ferry, *Egremont*
Salcombe
Contact telephone: 01584-531775
The club is an *RYA* recognised sailing school. It has been based in Salcombe since 1955. As well as organizing courses, the club welcomes cruisers to its floating clubhouse. You can enjoy a hot shower or stay longer for a drink or meal. The club has a fleet of boats on which members and guests can cruise or do a practical course. If you can come alongside with your dinghy, you will find a warm welcome. The Bistro is open from May to September.

Mayflower Sailing Club
Email: mayflowersc@hotmail.com
Home Page: www.mayflowersc.org.uk
Contact Denise Ramsey on 01752-662256
This is a dinghy sailing club that has a policy of introducing people to the sport of sailing,

Plym Yacht Club
Langs House. The Quay,
Oreston, Plymouth PL9 7NE
Tel: 01752-404991
Homepage: www.plymyachtclub.org.uk
Founded in 1970, the clubhouse overlooks the moorings and Oreston Green. The dock, of the same name, in front of the quay was filled in to provide open public space The club has an active racing and cruising membership and hosts many events, like the Plymouth Boat Rally. In 2002 the club hosts the National Osprey championships. There is also a winter social programme. Enquiries regarding membership, sailing or moorings are welcome. Visitors requesting a temporary mooring for boats below 35 feet should telephone the club to be advised on availability. Facilities include a bar, showers, moorings and slipway. Food is available after racing on Friday nights and a galley service is available in the season.

Royal Plymouth Corinthian YC
Madeira Road, Plymouth, PL1 2NY
Tel: 01752-664327
Email: secretary@rpcyc.demon.co.uk
Overlooking the Sound, the imposing building watches over the comings and goings of Plymouth. The club hosts national dinghy meetings and supports an active cruising section. There are two

moorings in front of the club that are available by arrangement and visitors are made welcome. The clubhouse has been refurbished and extended in the last couple of years and a lift for the disabled has been installed! The latter shows the progressive attitude of the club that is hosting the UK Laser Championships in 2002. The private harbour, dinghy park and slip are part of the facilities which include a restaurant, bar and showers. Also, there is a cadet room for the cadet members.

Royal Western Yacht Club of England
Queen Anne's Battery
Plymouth PL4 0TW
Tel: 01753-660077
Founded early in the 19th century, the modern clubhouse overlooking the marina belies the club's history. As a pioneer of ocean racing, OSTAR, Round Britain Double-Hander, etc. and the finish of the Fastnet Race, the club had a pivotal role in the development of the sport. Facilities include a daily restaurant service, hot and cold buffet in the bar, as well as most of the facilities one would expect of the senior club in Plymouth.

Salcombe Yacht Club
Cliff Road
Salcombe
Devon TQ8 8JQ
Tel: 01548-842593
The club was founded in 1895 and the luxurious premises overlook the moorings. Visitors can enjoy a drink or a meal on the patio whilst taking in one of Devon's finest seascapes. The club is steeped in the traditions of yachting, although its modern approach ensures a warm welcome is extended to visiting yachtsmen and women. The realistic prices of the food and drink make it the first stop for many regular visitors to Salcombe.

Saltash Sailing Club
Club House,
Waterside,
Saltash,
Cornwall
Tel: 01752-845988
Overlooked by the twin Tamar bridges to the north, the club offers a full sailing programme, for dinghies and cruisers. The club has a comfortable bar, and food in the season. Visiting yachtsmen can be offered a temporary mooring. Contact Mike Way the club administrator for further details,

Tamar River Sailing Club
883 Wolsley Road
St Budeaux
Plymouth
DevonPL5 1JX
For information Tel: 01752-795681
Hon. Sec: Mr Philip Garlick
Email:
philip@derringtondesign.freeserve.co.uk
Located on the east bank of the Tamar just south of the bridges, the club activities include cruising, racing and social events. The friendly club has recently extended the quay and refurbished the clubhouse. Another facility that has enhanced the club is the 20 m plus floating pontoon that can be used for temporary mooring at all states of the tide. Built with National Lottery funding and incorporating a hoist to assist the disabled, it has become a showpiece of how the sport can attract and keep the physically challenged. They have moorings, storage and liftout for

members. The club is open 1200 – 1900 on Saturdays and 1930 – 2300 on Fridays during the winter. In the season the club is open longer hours to coincide with the club's cruiser racing programme on Mondays and Saturdays.

Torpoint Mosquito Sailing Club
Off Marine Drive
Torpoint
Devon
For information telephone 01752-812508
The club is probably best known in recent times as a club involved in catamaran development. Pete Goss is one name associated with the club. This is an active racing club with races on Monday, Tuesday and Saturday during the season. The bar is open most evenings. The club has showers and toilets and makes visiting yachtsmen welcome.

Weir Quay Sailing Club
Hon. Secretary,
25 Chestnut Lane,
Tavistock PL19 9JJ
For information telephone: 01822614769
Email: dstjsemken@aol.com or
weirquays@eurobell.co.uk
The club is near the villages of Bere Ferrers and Bere Alston on the east bank of the Tamar. It is near the progressive Weir Quay boatyard. The enlarged club facilities include a bar, showers, toilets and some drying moorings.

Yealm Yacht Club
Riverside Road East
Newton Ferrers
Plymouth
Devon PL8 1AE
Tel: 01752-872291
The club is open every evening from 1830 – 2230, except Sundays in winter. You will find a warm welcome at lunchtimes from 1200 – 1500. There are changing facilities and showers that can be used out of hours by asking at Tubbs the Chemist near the club, to buy a token. In the summer and most nights in the winter the club operates a continental-style restaurant, although booking is advisable, tel: 01752-872232 to make a reservation. There is table tennis and pool in the bar for the more recreational visitor. Alternatively, you can admire the tranquil setting of Noss Mayo across the Newton Arm. When the tide is right it is a pleasant trip in the dinghy up to the club, with not too far to go when returning to the moorings in the Pool.

Cruising Association
Whilst this is not a local club, it has an active presence in Plymouth. Members may like to contact the Honorary Local Representative (LHR) for the port of Plymouth, Mr Edward Cartner. He can be contacted on 01752-491616 and will be pleased to answer any questions.

Programme of Maritime Events, Plymouth 2002

Bettinson Plymouth to Falmouth Yacht Race	May 4	RWYC
J24 Spring Cup	May 4/5/6	RWYC
Bettinson Fowey to Plymouth Yacht Race	May 6	RWYC
Plymouth to Salcombe Single-handed Race	May 11	RNSA
Keith Hyde Memorial Yacht Race	May 12	PYC
Inter-Services RS Asymmetrical Championships	May 18/19	PYC/RNSA
Hands Deep Yacht Race	May 25	SSC
Plymouth to St Peter Port Yacht Race	May 31	RNSA
Plymouth to Fowey Single-handed Yacht Race	June 1	RNSA
Asymmetrical Open Meeting	June 1/2	MSC
Plymouth Multihull Grand Priz	June 1/2	RPCYC
Royal Princess in Plymouth Sound	June 7	
Bond Pearce Plymouth to St Malo Yacht Race	June 13	RWYC
Plymouth to Fowey Double-handed Yacht Race	June 22	RWYC
RNLI Passage Yacht Race to River Yealm	June 22	YYC
Plymouth Mirror Challenge	June 23/30	RPCYC
Plymouth to Trebeurden Yacht Race	June 27	YYC
Plymouth to Dartmouth Single-handed Yacht Race	July 5	RNSA
Volvo RYA South West Zone Dinghy Champs	July 6/7	PYC

Royal Princess in Plymouth Sound	July 6	
Bosun National Championships	July 13/14	RNSA
UIM Class 1 World Offshore Powerboat Event	July 19/21	
Laser/Laser Radial National Championships	July 21/28	RPCYC
Brilliance of the Seas in Cawsand Bay	July 24	
Plymouth to San Sebastian Yacht Race	July 28	RWYC
Scott Bader Port of Plymouth Regatta	July 30/Aug 3	PPSA
Plymouth Maritime Festival	August 2/ 4	
Osprey Open National Championships	August 3/9	PYC
Trawler Race	August 4	
Classic Boat Rally	August 4/5	PYC
Classic Boat Race to Fowey	August 6	PYC
Plymouth to Fowey Yacht Race	August 10	SSC
Fowey to Plymouth Yacht Race	August 11	PYC
Yealm Regatta	Aug 17/18	YYC
Silouette Rally & National Championships	Aug 17/23	RPCYC
Plymouth Navy Days	August 24/26	
Europa in Plymouth Sound	August 30	
European Water Ski Racing Championships	Aug 31 to Sept 5	
Laser II and National 12 Open Meeting	Aug 31/Sept 1	SSC
175th Anniversary Yacht Races & Sailpast	Sept 5/6/7	RWYC

Salcombe to Plymouth Yacht Race	Sept 8	RWYC
OCRDA Powerboat Grand Prix	Sept 14/15	
Cargreen Regatta Yacht Race	Sept 21	

Key:

MSC Mayflower Sailing Club	PYC
Royal Naval Sailing Association	RNSA
Royal Plymouth Corinthian Yacht Club	RPCYC
Poyal Western Yacht Club of England	RWYC
Saltash Sailing Club	SSC
Yealm Yacht Club	YYC

Non-Maritime Event

National Fireworks Competition	Aug 6/7

Bibliography

Charts listed in the text
River Yealm Harbour, D & M Journals, 2001
Salcombe Harbour Guide 2001, Salcombe Harbour Authority
The Shell Pilot of the English Channel 1 Capt. C Coote, Faber & Faber, 1987
Various articles published published by IPC and Future Publishing
Water Events Diary 2002,Queen's Harbour Master, Plymouth
Waterfront Plymouth, R Brimacombe, Mor Marketing 2000
PBO Small Craft Almanac 2001
Macmillan Reeds Channel Almanac 2001

Tides and Ads

The tidal predictions for the Port of Devonport have been computed and supplied by the UK Hydrographic Office and are Crown Copyright. These tide tables of Falmouth are **"Reproduced from Admiralty Tide Tables by permission of the Controller of Her Majesty's Stationery Office and the UK Hydrographic Office."**

For BST please add one hour during the appropriate months. Mariners are reminded that they are only predictions and are subject to changes due to meteorological conditions, especially in shallow waters. High pressure can reduce the high water level. Low pressure may produce tidal levels higher than those predicted. Whilst every care has been made in compiling the Tide Tables, the publishers or the UKHO cannot not be held responsible for any inaccuracies.

Approximate time differences of HW at some locations:

Plymouth Sound	- 6 minutes
Cargreen	+ 5 minutes
River Yealm	+ 6 minutes
Salcombe	+10 minutes
Looe	- 10 minutes
Fowey	- 12 minutes
Falmouth	- 25 minutes
Dartmouth	+30 minutes
Dover	-5 hours 45 minutes

For those with Internet access try the following URL for FREE tidal information worldwide. www.easytide.com It provides the full harmonic movement for the next seven days

This section contains a list of advertisers arranged alphabetically to match the tidal predictions.

AQUA-TECH MARINE LTD

Stainless & Aluminium Marine Fittings

Pulpits•Pushpits•Stanchions•ChainPlates•Stem Head Rollers•Fuel & Water Tanks•Stainless Steel Welding & Polishing•Aluminium Fabrications•Spray Hoods & Fittings in Stock

24A Commercial Road
Coxside
Plymouth PL4 0LE
Tel/Fax: 01752 228751
Mobile: 07980 802933

Bridgend Boat Company Ltd

BRIDGEND BOAT COMPANY LTD

FOR QUALITY REPAIRS FITTING OUT & BOAT BUILDING ONE-STOP SHOP

Western Hangar
Mount Batten
Plymouth PL9 9SJ

Tel: 01752 404082
Fax: 01752 403405
Email: bboatsco@aol.com

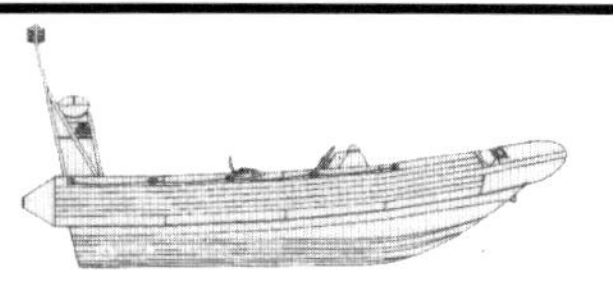

Inflatable Boat Services (Falmouth) Ltd

inc. South West Liferafts

Servicing•Sales•Repair•Hire

dinghies • ribs • liferafts
life jackets • accessories

new & second hand
part exchange welcome

visit our new showroom and workshop

89 North Parade, Falmouth
(opposite Falmouth Marina)
Tel: 01326 313800 Fax: 01326 313338
Email: info@inflatableboatservices.co.uk

Inshore sails & covers

makers of quality canopies, sprayhoods & covers
sail repairs

Tamar Building, Q.A.B. Marina
Coxside, Plymouth PL4 0LP
Tel: 01752 229661
Fax: 01752 611509

ENGLAND — PLYMOUTH (DEVONPORT)

LAT 50°22'N LONG 4°11'W

TIME ZONE **UT(GMT)** TIMES AND HEIGHTS OF HIGH AND LOW WATERS YEAR **2002**

JANUARY

Day	Time	m
1 TU	0045 0654 1312 1922	0.9 5.5 0.8 5.3
2 W	0130 0740 1358 2008	0.9 5.6 0.8 5.2
3 TH	0215 0826 1444 2055	1.0 5.5 0.9 5.2
4 F	0300 0912 1531 2143	1.1 5.4 1.1 5.0
5 SA	0347 1001 1619 2235	1.3 5.2 1.3 4.8
6 SU	0438 1055 1714 2334	1.5 5.0 1.5 4.7
7 M	0537 1158 1819	1.8 4.8 1.7
8 TU	0042 0649 1309 1933	4.6 1.9 4.7 1.8
9 W	0152 0807 1419 2046	4.6 1.9 4.7 1.8
10 TH	0257 0916 1523 2148	4.7 1.7 4.8 1.6
11 F	0354 1014 1619 2240	4.9 1.5 4.9 1.4
12 SA	0444 1105 1708 2326	5.1 1.3 5.0 1.2
13 SU ●	0528 1150 1751	5.2 1.1 5.1
14 M	0008 0606 1232 1829	1.2 5.3 1.1 5.1
15 TU	0047 0642 1310 1904	1.1 5.3 1.1 5.0
16 W	0122 0716 1345 1937	1.2 5.3 1.2 5.0
17 TH	0154 0749 1416 2010	1.3 5.2 1.3 4.9
18 F	0222 0824 1444 2044	1.4 5.1 1.4 4.8
19 SA	0249 0858 1512 2119	1.6 5.0 1.6 4.6
20 SU	0317 0934 1543 2156	1.7 4.8 1.8 4.5
21 M	0351 1012 1622 2240	1.9 4.6 1.9 4.4
22 TU	0438 1100 1719 2337	2.1 4.5 2.1 4.3
23 W	0550 1202 1836	2.2 4.4 2.1
24 TH	0049 0714 1319 1950	4.3 2.2 4.4 2.0
25 F	0209 0827 1441 2058	4.4 2.0 4.5 1.8
26 SA	0319 0932 1548 2159	4.7 1.7 4.7 1.5
27 SU	0416 1031 1644 2255	5.0 1.3 5.0 1.2
28 M ○	0507 1125 1736 2347	5.3 1.0 5.2 0.9
29 TU	0555 1216 1825	5.5 0.7 5.3
30 W	0036 0642 1305 1913	0.7 5.6 0.5 5.4
31 TH	0123 0730 1351 2000	0.6 5.7 0.4 5.4

FEBRUARY

Day	Time	m
1 F	0207 0817 1435 2044	0.6 5.7 0.5 5.4
2 SA	0249 0901 1516 2127	0.7 5.6 0.7 5.2
3 SU	0330 0945 1557 2210	0.9 5.4 1.0 5.0
4 M	0412 1030 1641 2258	1.2 5.1 1.3 4.7
5 TU	0500 1122 1732 2357	1.6 4.7 1.7 4.5
6 W	0600 1230 1839	1.9 4.5 2.0
7 TH	0112 0722 1349 2011	4.4 2.1 4.3 2.1
8 F	0228 0854 1502 2130	4.4 2.0 4.4 1.9
9 SA	0332 1002 1603 2228	4.6 1.7 4.6 1.6
10 SU	0426 1054 1653 2314	4.9 1.4 4.8 1.4
11 M	0510 1138 1735 2356	5.1 1.2 4.9 1.2
12 TU ●	0549 1218 1812	5.2 1.0 5.0
13 W	0033 0624 1255 1846	1.0 5.3 0.9 5.1
14 TH	0107 0659 1327 1919	1.0 5.3 0.9 5.1
15 F	0136 0732 1355 1951	1.0 5.3 1.0 5.0
16 SA	0201 0805 1419 2022	1.1 5.2 1.1 4.9
17 SU	0223 0836 1441 2051	1.2 5.0 1.3 4.8
18 M	0246 0903 1505 2118	1.4 4.9 1.4 4.7
19 TU	0313 0930 1536 2149	1.6 4.7 1.6 4.5
20 W	0350 1008 1618 2238	1.8 4.5 1.9 4.4
21 TH	0443 1108 1725 2348	2.1 4.3 2.1 4.2
22 F	0617 1228 1906	2.2 4.2 2.2
23 SA	0116 0753 1405 2029	4.3 2.1 4.3 2.0
24 SU	0247 0909 1528 2140	4.6 1.7 4.6 1.6
25 M	0354 1015 1628 2241	4.9 1.3 4.9 1.1
26 TU	0448 1112 1720 2334	5.3 0.8 5.2 0.7
27 W ○	0538 1203 1809	5.6 0.4 5.4
28 TH	0023 0626 1250 1856	0.4 5.8 0.2 5.5

MARCH

Day	Time	m
1 F	0109 0714 1335 1941	0.2 5.8 0.1 5.6
2 SA	0151 0759 1416 2024	0.2 5.8 0.2 5.5
3 SU	0230 0842 1454 2103	0.3 5.7 0.4 5.4
4 M	0308 0922 1531 2140	0.6 5.4 0.8 5.1
5 TU	0346 1001 1609 2217	1.0 5.0 1.3 4.8
6 W	0428 1044 1654 2304	1.5 4.6 1.8 4.4
7 TH	0522 1152 1754	2.0 4.2 2.2
8 F	0031 0640 1327 1929	4.2 2.3 4.1 2.4
9 SA	0202 0838 1444 2115	4.2 2.2 4.2 2.2
10 SU	0311 0948 1545 2211	4.5 1.8 4.4 1.8
11 M	0404 1037 1634 2256	4.8 1.4 4.7 1.4
12 TU	0448 1119 1713 2335	5.0 1.1 4.9 1.1
13 W	0526 1157 1749	5.2 0.9 5.0
14 TH ●	0011 0601 1232 1823	0.9 5.3 0.8 5.1
15 F	0044 0636 1302 1855	0.9 5.3 0.8 5.1
16 SA	0111 0710 1327 1927	0.9 5.3 0.9 5.1
17 SU	0135 0742 1350 1956	1.0 5.2 1.0 5.0
18 M	0157 0810 1412 2022	1.1 5.1 1.1 4.9
19 TU	0219 0835 1436 2046	1.2 4.9 1.3 4.8
20 W	0246 0900 1504 2115	1.4 4.7 1.5 4.7
21 TH	0320 0938 1543 2202	1.6 4.5 1.8 4.5
22 F	0410 1040 1643 2313	1.9 4.3 2.1 4.3
23 SA	0538 1201 1832	2.2 4.1 2.3
24 SU	0041 0728 1342 2006	4.3 2.1 4.2 2.0
25 M	0219 0851 1510 2122	4.6 1.7 4.6 1.6
26 TU	0332 0958 1610 2224	5.0 1.1 5.0 1.1
27 W	0428 1054 1701 2316	5.3 0.7 5.3 0.6
28 TH ○	0518 1143 1748	5.6 0.3 5.5
29 F	0003 0605 1230 1834	0.3 5.8 0.1 5.6
30 SA	0048 0652 1312 1918	0.1 5.8 0.0 5.7
31 SU	0129 0737 1352 1958	0.1 5.8 0.2 5.6

APRIL

Day	Time	m
1 M	0208 0818 1429 2035	0.3 5.6 0.5 5.4
2 TU	0244 0856 1505 2108	0.6 5.3 0.9 5.1
3 W	0321 0931 1541 2137	1.1 4.9 1.4 4.8
4 TH	0402 1008 1624 2214	1.6 4.5 1.9 4.5
5 F	0454 1109 1722 2327	2.0 4.1 2.3 4.2
6 SA	0608 1304 1848	2.3 4.0 2.5
7 SU	0132 0810 1420 2044	4.2 2.3 4.1 2.3
8 M	0242 0921 1519 2142	4.4 1.9 4.4 1.9
9 TU	0335 1008 1605 2226	4.7 1.5 4.7 1.5
10 W	0418 1049 1644 2305	4.9 1.2 4.9 1.2
11 TH	0457 1126 1720 2341	5.1 1.0 5.0 1.0
12 F ●	0533 1159 1754	5.2 0.8 5.1
13 SA	0012 0609 1229 1828	0.9 5.2 0.8 5.2
14 SU	0041 0644 1256 1900	0.9 5.2 0.9 5.2
15 M	0107 0717 1322 1930	0.9 5.2 1.0 5.1
16 TU	0132 0746 1347 1957	1.0 5.0 1.1 5.1
17 W	0158 0814 1414 2024	1.1 4.9 1.3 4.9
18 TH	0228 0845 1445 2059	1.3 4.7 1.5 4.8
19 F	0305 0928 1527 2148	1.6 4.5 1.8 4.6
20 SA	0358 1028 1630 2254	1.9 4.3 2.1 4.4
21 SU	0527 1147 1812	2.1 4.2 2.2
22 M	0018 0707 1325 1944	4.4 1.9 4.3 2.0
23 TU	0154 0829 1447 2059	4.6 1.6 4.6 1.5
24 W	0307 0935 1547 2200	5.0 1.1 5.0 1.1
25 TH	0404 1030 1637 2253	5.3 0.7 5.3 0.6
26 F	0455 1119 1724 2340	5.6 0.3 5.5 0.4
27 SA ○	0543 1205 1809	5.7 0.2 5.6
28 SU	0024 0629 1248 1852	0.2 5.7 0.2 5.6
29 M	0106 0713 1328 1932	0.3 5.6 0.4 5.5
30 TU	0145 0754 1405 2008	0.5 5.4 0.7 5.4

ENGLAND — PLYMOUTH (DEVONPORT)

LAT 50°22'N LONG 4°11'W

TIME ZONE **UT(GMT)** TIMES AND HEIGHTS OF HIGH AND LOW WATERS YEAR **2002**

MAY

Day	Time	m	Day	Time	m
1 W	0223 0832 1442 2038	0.8 5.1 1.1 5.1	**16** TH	0146 0802 1403 2012	1.1 4.9 1.3 5.1
2 TH	0301 0906 1519 2107	1.2 4.8 1.5 4.8	**17** F	0223 0840 1440 2052	1.3 4.8 1.5 4.9
3 F	0342 0941 1602 2144	1.6 4.4 2.0 4.5	**18** SA	0306 0926 1528 2142	1.5 4.6 1.7 4.8
4 SA	0433 1035 1657 2242	2.0 4.1 2.3 4.3	**19** SU	0403 1024 1633 2243	1.7 4.4 1.9 4.6
5 SU	0539 1226 1809	2.2 4.0 2.4	**20** M	0520 1137 1755	1.8 4.4 2.0
6 M	0043 0706 1342 1939	4.2 2.2 4.1 2.3	**21** TU	0000 0644 1303 1917	4.6 1.7 4.4 1.8
7 TU	0159 0830 1439 2052	4.3 2.0 4.3 2.0	**22** W	0125 0800 1417 2030	4.7 1.5 4.7 1.5
8 W	0254 0923 1526 2142	4.6 1.6 4.6 1.7	**23** TH	0237 0906 1518 2132	5.0 1.2 5.0 1.2
9 TH	0340 1006 1606 2224	4.8 1.4 4.8 1.4	**24** F	0337 1003 1611 2226	5.2 0.8 5.2 0.9
10 F	0421 1045 1645 2302	5.0 1.1 5.0 1.2	**25** SA	0430 1054 1659 2316	5.4 0.6 5.4 0.6
11 SA	0501 1120 1722 2336	5.1 1.0 5.1 1.0	**26** SU ○	0520 1141 1745	5.5 0.5 5.5
12 SU ●	0540 1153 1759	5.1 1.0 5.2	**27** M	0001 0607 1225 1828	0.5 5.4 0.5 5.5
13 M	0009 0617 1226 1834	1.0 5.1 1.0 5.2	**28** TU	0045 0651 1306 1908	0.6 5.4 0.7 5.4
14 TU	0041 0654 1258 1907	1.0 5.1 1.0 5.2	**29** W	0126 0734 1345 1944	0.7 5.2 0.9 5.3
15 W	0113 0728 1329 1938	1.0 5.0 1.1 5.1	**30** TH	0206 0812 1423 2016	1.0 5.0 1.2 5.1
			31 F	0245 0847 1501 2047	1.3 4.7 1.6 4.9

JUNE

Day	Time	m	Day	Time	m
1 SA	0325 0923 1542 2125	1.6 4.5 1.9 4.7	**16** SU	0312 0927 1532 2138	1.2 4.8 1.4 5.0
2 SU	0411 1009 1630 2215	1.9 4.2 2.1 4.5	**17** M	0405 1020 1627 2234	1.4 4.7 1.6 4.9
3 M	0505 1116 1728 2321	2.1 4.1 2.3 4.3	**18** TU	0505 1123 1732 2340	1.5 4.6 1.7 4.8
4 TU	0608 1236 1834	2.1 4.1 2.3	**19** W	0614 1233 1843	1.5 4.6 1.7
5 W	0046 0713 1341 1940	4.3 2.0 4.3 2.1	**20** TH	0054 0725 1343 1955	4.8 1.5 4.7 1.6
6 TH	0155 0815 1434 2040	4.4 1.8 4.5 1.9	**21** F	0206 0834 1446 2102	4.8 1.4 4.8 1.4
7 F	0251 0908 1522 2132	4.6 1.6 4.7 1.6	**22** SA	0310 0936 1544 2202	4.9 1.2 5.0 1.2
8 SA	0340 0955 1607 2218	4.8 1.4 4.9 1.4	**23** SU	0408 1031 1636 2255	5.1 1.0 5.2 1.0
9 SU	0427 1038 1650 2300	4.9 1.2 5.0 1.2	**24** M ○	0500 1120 1724 2343	5.1 0.9 5.3 0.9
10 M ●	0511 1119 1731 2340	5.0 1.1 5.1 1.1	**25** TU	0549 1206 1808	5.2 0.9 5.3
11 TU	0553 1159 1811	5.0 1.1 5.2	**26** W	0029 0634 1250 1848	0.8 5.1 0.9 5.3
12 W	0020 0634 1239 1849	1.0 5.0 1.1 5.2	**27** TH	0112 0716 1330 1925	0.9 5.0 1.1 5.2
13 TH	0101 0715 1319 1927	1.0 5.0 1.1 5.2	**28** F	0152 0755 1408 1959	1.0 4.9 1.2 5.1
14 F	0142 0756 1400 2007	1.0 5.0 1.2 5.2	**29** SA	0230 0830 1444 2032	1.2 4.7 1.4 5.0
15 SA	0225 0840 1444 2050	1.1 4.9 1.3 5.1	**30** SU	0307 0904 1520 2108	1.4 4.6 1.6 4.8

JULY

Day	Time	m	Day	Time	m
1 M	0343 0942 1557 2148	1.6 4.5 1.8 4.7	**16** TU	0353 1008 1611 2220	1.0 4.9 1.2 5.1
2 TU	0424 1027 1640 2236	1.8 4.3 2.0 4.5	**17** W	0442 1100 1703 2315	1.2 4.7 1.5 4.9
3 W	0512 1121 1734 2332	2.0 4.2 2.1 4.4	**18** TH	0539 1200 1805	1.5 4.6 1.7
4 TH	0609 1225 1837	2.0 4.2 2.2	**19** F	0021 0646 1309 1918	4.7 1.7 4.6 1.8
5 F	0040 0710 1332 1940	4.3 2.0 4.3 2.1	**20** SA	0136 0801 1418 2035	4.6 1.7 4.6 1.7
6 SA	0153 0811 1434 2040	4.4 1.8 4.5 1.9	**21** SU	0248 0913 1522 2144	4.6 1.6 4.8 1.6
7 SU	0258 0908 1530 2137	4.5 1.7 4.7 1.6	**22** M	0351 1015 1618 2242	4.7 1.4 5.0 1.3
8 M	0354 1001 1620 2229	4.7 1.4 4.9 1.4	**23** TU	0446 1107 1708 2332	4.9 1.2 5.1 1.1
9 TU	0445 1051 1706 2318	4.9 1.3 5.1 1.2	**24** W ○	0534 1154 1751	5.0 1.1 5.2
10 W ●	0533 1139 1751	5.0 1.1 5.2	**25** TH	0017 0618 1237 1831	1.0 5.0 1.0 5.3
11 TH	0005 0618 1227 1834	1.0 5.1 1.0 5.3	**26** F	0100 0658 1316 1907	0.9 5.0 1.0 5.3
12 F	0052 0705 1313 1918	0.8 5.1 0.9 5.4	**27** SA	0138 0734 1351 1940	1.0 4.9 1.1 5.2
13 SA	0138 0751 1357 2002	0.8 5.1 0.9 5.4	**28** SU	0211 0807 1423 2013	1.1 4.9 1.2 5.1
14 SU	0223 0836 1441 2046	0.8 5.1 0.9 5.4	**29** M	0242 0839 1451 2046	1.2 4.8 1.4 5.0
15 M	0308 0921 1525 2132	0.9 5.0 1.1 5.3	**30** TU	0309 0912 1518 2119	1.4 4.7 1.6 4.8
			31 W	0337 0947 1546 2154	1.6 4.5 1.8 4.6

AUGUST

Day	Time	m	Day	Time	m
1 TH	0410 1027 1623 2235	1.8 4.4 2.0 4.5	**16** F	0502 1125 1729 2349	1.6 4.6 1.8 4.5
2 F	0457 1117 1723 2330	2.0 4.3 2.2 4.3	**17** SA	0605 1237 1844	1.9 4.4 2.1
3 SA	0607 1223 1845	2.1 4.2 2.2	**18** SU	0113 0732 1356 2019	4.3 2.1 4.4 2.1
4 SU	0045 0722 1342 1959	4.2 2.1 4.3 2.1	**19** M	0235 0902 1507 2136	4.4 2.0 4.6 1.8
5 M	0215 0831 1455 2105	4.3 1.9 4.6 1.8	**20** TU	0342 1006 1605 2233	4.5 1.7 4.8 1.5
6 TU	0327 0933 1554 2205	4.6 1.6 4.8 1.5	**21** W	0435 1056 1653 2321	4.7 1.4 5.1 1.2
7 W	0424 1031 1645 2301	4.8 1.3 5.1 1.1	**22** TH ○	0520 1140 1734	4.9 1.1 5.2
8 TH ●	0515 1124 1732 2352	5.0 1.0 5.3 0.8	**23** F	0003 0559 1221 1810	1.0 5.0 1.0 5.3
9 F	0603 1214 1819	5.2 0.8 5.5	**24** SA	0042 0635 1257 1844	0.9 5.1 0.9 5.3
10 SA	0041 0650 1302 1905	0.6 5.3 0.6 5.6	**25** SU	0116 0708 1328 1917	0.9 5.1 1.0 5.3
11 SU	0127 0737 1346 1950	0.5 5.3 0.6 5.6	**26** M	0145 0739 1355 1948	1.0 5.0 1.1 5.2
12 M	0211 0821 1428 2034	0.4 5.3 0.6 5.6	**27** TU	0210 0809 1418 2019	1.1 5.0 1.3 5.1
13 TU	0252 0904 1508 2116	0.6 5.3 0.8 5.4	**28** W	0231 0839 1437 2047	1.3 4.8 1.4 4.9
14 W	0332 0946 1548 2159	0.8 5.1 1.0 5.2	**29** TH	0252 0908 1459 2114	1.5 4.7 1.6 4.7
15 TH	0414 1031 1633 2246	1.2 4.9 1.4 4.8	**30** F	0317 0939 1529 2147	1.7 4.5 1.9 4.5
			31 SA	0352 1021 1614 2238	1.9 4.4 2.1 4.3

ENGLAND — PLYMOUTH (DEVONPORT)

LAT 50°22'N LONG 4°11'W

TIME ZONE **UT(GMT)** TIMES AND HEIGHTS OF HIGH AND LOW WATERS YEAR 2002

SEPTEMBER

Day	Time	m	Day	Time	m
1	0449	2.2	**16**	0100	4.1
	1124	4.2		0710	2.4
SU	1742	2.4	M	1339	4.3
	2353	4.2		2014	2.3
2	0638	2.3	**17**	0226	4.2
	1248	4.3		0854	2.2
M	1926	2.3	TU	1452	4.5
				2128	1.9
3	0135	4.2	**18**	0331	4.5
	0803	2.1		0952	1.8
TU	1423	4.5	W	1549	4.8
	2042	1.9		2218	1.5
4	0308	4.5	**19**	0420	4.8
	0913	1.8		1038	1.4
W	1532	4.9	TH	1633	5.1
	2148	1.5		2301	1.2
5	0407	4.8	**20**	0500	5.0
	1014	1.3		1119	1.1
TH	1624	5.2	F	1711	5.3
	2245	1.0		2340	1.0
6	0457	5.1	**21**	0535	5.1
	1108	0.9		1156	1.0
F	1712	5.5	SA	1746	5.4
	2336	0.6	O		
7	0544	5.4	**22**	0015	0.8
	1157	0.6		0607	5.2
SA	1759	5.7	SU	1230	0.9
●				1818	5.4
8	0023	0.4	**23**	0047	0.9
	0630	5.5		0639	5.2
SU	1244	0.4	M	1259	1.0
	1845	5.8		1850	5.4
9	0108	0.2	**24**	0113	0.9
	0715	5.6		0709	5.2
M	1327	0.3	TU	1323	1.1
	1930	5.8		1921	5.3
10	0150	0.3	**25**	0135	1.1
	0758	5.6		0739	5.1
TU	1407	0.4	W	1344	1.2
	2013	5.7		1950	5.1
11	0229	0.5	**26**	0155	1.2
	0839	5.4		0807	5.0
W	1445	0.7	TH	1403	1.4
	2054	5.5		2017	5.0
12	0307	0.8	**27**	0216	1.4
	0919	5.2		0833	4.9
TH	1523	1.0	F	1426	1.6
	2134	5.1		2041	4.8
13	0345	1.3	**28**	0240	1.6
	0959	4.9		0901	4.7
F	1605	1.5	SA	1456	1.8
	2216	4.7		2114	4.6
14	0429	1.8	**29**	0314	1.9
	1047	4.6		0944	4.5
SA	1658	2.0	SU	1539	2.1
	2317	4.3		2208	4.3
15	0529	2.2	**30**	0405	2.3
	1206	4.3		1048	4.3
SU	1816	2.3	M	1654	2.4
				2325	4.1

OCTOBER

Day	Time	m	Day	Time	m
1	0557	2.5	**16**	0206	4.2
	1210	4.3		0829	2.4
TU	1900	2.4	W	1427	4.5
				2103	2.0
2	0107	4.2	**17**	0307	4.5
	0739	2.3		0925	2.0
W	1351	4.5	TH	1521	4.8
	2022	1.9		2151	1.6
3	0248	4.5	**18**	0353	4.8
	0854	1.8		1009	1.6
TH	1507	4.9	F	1605	5.1
	2129	1.4		2231	1.3
4	0347	4.9	**19**	0431	5.0
	0955	1.3		1048	1.3
F	1602	5.3	SA	1642	5.2
	2224	0.9		2308	1.1
5	0436	5.3	**20**	0505	5.2
	1048	0.9		1124	1.1
SA	1650	5.6	SU	1716	5.3
	2314	0.5		2342	1.0
6	0521	5.5	**21**	0537	5.3
	1136	0.5		1157	1.0
SU	1737	5.8	M	1750	5.4
●			O		
7	0000	0.3	**22**	0012	1.0
	0605	5.7		0609	5.3
M	1221	0.3	TU	1226	1.0
	1822	5.9		1823	5.3
8	0044	0.2	**23**	0038	1.0
	0650	5.7		0641	5.3
TU	1303	0.3	W	1252	1.1
	1907	5.9		1855	5.3
9	0125	0.3	**24**	0103	1.1
	0732	5.7		0712	5.3
W	1343	0.4	TH	1315	1.2
	1950	5.7		1925	5.2
10	0204	0.6	**25**	0126	1.3
	0813	5.5		0740	5.1
TH	1422	0.7	F	1339	1.4
	2031	5.4		1953	5.0
11	0241	1.0	**26**	0150	1.5
	0850	5.3		0808	5.0
F	1500	1.2	SA	1406	1.6
	2109	5.0		2022	4.8
12	0318	1.5	**27**	0218	1.7
	0927	5.0		0840	4.9
SA	1542	1.7	SU	1439	1.8
	2148	4.6		2100	4.6
13	0402	2.0	**28**	0255	2.0
	1009	4.6		0925	4.7
SU	1635	2.1	M	1524	2.1
	2248	4.2		2155	4.4
14	0502	2.4	**29**	0348	2.3
	1130	4.3		1027	4.5
M	1752	2.5	TU	1641	2.3
				2307	4.2
15	0044	4.1	**30**	0529	2.5
	0641	2.6		1144	4.5
TU	1316	4.3	W	1833	2.3
	1955	2.4			
			31	0042	4.3
				0712	2.3
			TH	1317	4.6
				1956	1.9

NOVEMBER

Day	Time	m	Day	Time	m
1	0218	4.6	**16**	0313	4.7
	0828	1.9		0928	1.8
F	1436	5.0	SA	1526	4.9
	2103	1.4		2151	1.6
2	0320	5.0	**17**	0354	4.9
	0930	1.4		1009	1.5
SA	1535	5.3	SU	1606	5.1
	2159	1.0		2229	1.3
3	0410	5.3	**18**	0430	5.1
	1023	1.0		1047	1.3
SU	1626	5.6	M	1644	5.2
	2249	0.6		2304	1.2
4	0456	5.6	**19**	0506	5.2
	1111	0.6		1122	1.2
M	1714	5.8	TU	1721	5.2
●	2336	0.4		2336	1.1
5	0542	5.7	**20**	0541	5.3
	1157	0.5		1154	1.2
TU	1800	5.8	W	1758	5.2
			O		
6	0019	0.4	**21**	0006	1.2
	0625	5.8		0616	5.3
W	1241	0.5	TH	1225	1.2
	1845	5.7		1833	5.2
7	0101	0.5	**22**	0037	1.2
	0708	5.7		0649	5.3
TH	1322	0.6	F	1255	1.3
	1929	5.6		1907	5.1
8	0141	0.8	**23**	0107	1.3
	0748	5.6		0721	5.2
F	1402	0.9	SA	1326	1.4
	2010	5.3		1939	5.0
9	0219	1.2	**24**	0138	1.4
	0826	5.3		0754	5.1
SA	1442	1.3	SU	1400	1.5
	2049	5.0		2014	4.9
10	0258	1.6	**25**	0212	1.6
	0902	5.0		0831	5.0
SU	1525	1.7	M	1439	1.7
	2129	4.6		2056	4.7
11	0342	2.1	**26**	0254	1.9
	0942	4.7		0917	4.9
M	1616	2.1	TU	1528	1.9
	2223	4.3		2148	4.5
12	0437	2.4	**27**	0349	2.1
	1043	4.5		1013	4.8
TU	1723	2.4	W	1636	2.0
				2253	4.4
13	0007	4.1	**28**	0507	2.2
	0553	2.6		1122	4.7
W	1231	4.4	TH	1801	2.0
	1856	2.4			
14	0126	4.2	**29**	0013	4.4
	0732	2.5		0635	2.1
TH	1344	4.5	F	1241	4.8
	2016	2.2		1921	1.8
15	0226	4.4	**30**	0137	4.6
	0839	2.2		0753	1.9
F	1440	4.7	SA	1358	4.9
	2108	1.8		2031	1.5

DECEMBER

Day	Time	m	Day	Time	m
1	0244	4.9	**16**	0307	4.7
	0859	1.5		0919	1.9
SU	1504	5.2	M	1523	4.8
	2131	1.2		2141	1.7
2	0341	5.2	**17**	0352	4.9
	0956	1.2		1005	1.7
M	1600	5.4	TU	1610	4.9
	2224	0.9		2223	1.5
3	0432	5.4	**18**	0435	5.1
	1048	0.9		1046	1.5
TU	1652	5.5	W	1654	5.0
	2313	0.8		2302	1.3
4	0519	5.6	**19**	0516	5.2
	1136	0.7		1125	1.3
W	1741	5.6	TH	1736	5.1
●	2359	0.7	O	2341	1.3
5	0605	5.6	**20**	0555	5.3
	1221	0.7		1204	1.2
TH	1828	5.5	F	1817	5.1
6	0042	0.8	**21**	0019	1.2
	0648	5.6		0633	5.3
F	1306	0.8	SA	1243	1.2
	1912	5.4		1855	5.1
7	0124	1.0	**22**	0057	1.2
	0730	5.5		0711	5.3
SA	1348	1.0	SU	1322	1.2
	1955	5.2		1934	5.0
8	0204	1.3	**23**	0135	1.3
	0809	5.3		0749	5.3
SU	1430	1.3	M	1402	1.3
	2035	4.9		2013	5.0
9	0244	1.6	**24**	0215	1.4
	0845	5.1		0829	5.2
M	1512	1.6	TU	1444	1.4
	2113	4.7		2056	4.9
10	0325	1.9	**25**	0258	1.5
	0923	4.9		0913	5.1
TU	1556	1.9	W	1530	1.5
	2156	4.4		2143	4.8
11	0411	2.2	**26**	0346	1.7
	1009	4.7		1002	5.0
W	1646	2.1	TH	1623	1.6
	2253	4.3		2237	4.7
12	0506	2.4	**27**	0443	1.8
	1109	4.5		1059	4.9
TH	1746	2.3	F	1725	1.7
				2341	4.6
13	0009	4.2	**28**	0552	1.9
	0611	2.4		1206	4.8
F	1226	4.4	SA	1837	1.8
	1853	2.2			
14	0119	4.3	**29**	0053	4.6
	0722	2.3		0710	1.9
SA	1335	4.5	SU	1320	4.8
	1958	2.1		1952	1.7
15	0217	4.5	**30**	0206	4.7
	0826	2.1		0825	1.7
SU	1432	4.6	M	1432	4.9
	2054	1.9		2101	1.5
			31	0312	4.9
				0931	1.5
			TU	1538	5.0
				2202	1.3

ENGLAND — PLYMOUTH (DEVONPORT)

LAT 50°22'N LONG 4°11'W

TIME ZONE UT(GMT) — TIMES AND HEIGHTS OF HIGH AND LOW WATERS — YEAR 2003

JANUARY

	Time	m		Time	m
1	0410	5.2	16	0406	4.9
	1029	1.2		1014	1.6
W	1635	5.1	TH	1631	4.8
	2256	1.1		2235	1.5
2	0502	5.3	17	0453	5.1
	1121	1.0		1103	1.4
TH	1727	5.2	F	1718	5.0
●	2344	1.0		2322	1.3
3	0549	5.5	18	0537	5.2
	1210	0.9		1149	1.2
F	1816	5.2	SA	1803	5.1
			○		
4	0030	1.0	19	0007	1.1
	0633	5.5		0619	5.4
SA	1256	0.9	SU	1234	1.0
	1900	5.2		1846	5.1
5	0113	1.0	20	0050	1.0
	0715	5.5		0701	5.4
SU	1338	1.0	M	1318	0.9
	1942	5.1		1928	5.2
6	0153	1.1	21	0132	1.0
	0754	5.4		0743	5.5
M	1418	1.1	TU	1359	0.8
	2020	5.0		2009	5.2
7	0230	1.3	22	0213	1.0
	0829	5.2		0824	5.4
TU	1455	1.3	W	1440	0.9
	2053	4.8		2050	5.1
8	0305	1.5	23	0253	1.0
	0902	5.0		0905	5.4
W	1530	1.5	TH	1521	1.0
	2126	4.6		2131	5.0
9	0340	1.8	24	0334	1.2
	0938	4.8		0948	5.2
TH	1606	1.8	F	1603	1.2
	2204	4.5		2216	4.9
10	0418	2.0	25	0419	1.4
	1020	4.7		1036	5.0
F	1647	2.0	SA	1651	1.5
	2250	4.4		2308	4.7
11	0504	2.2	26	0513	1.7
	1110	4.5		1134	4.8
SA	1738	2.2	SU	1750	1.8
	2347	4.3			
12	0605	2.3	27	0014	4.5
	1212	4.4		0623	1.9
SU	1840	2.2	M	1247	4.6
				1908	1.9
13	0057	4.3	28	0132	4.5
	0713	2.3		0751	2.0
M	1325	4.4	TU	1408	4.5
	1945	2.1		2036	1.9
14	0210	4.4	29	0249	4.6
	0820	2.2		0914	1.8
TU	1437	4.5	W	1523	4.6
	2048	2.0		2149	1.7
15	0313	4.6	30	0355	4.9
	0921	1.9		1020	1.5
W	1538	4.6	TH	1626	4.8
	2144	1.7		2247	1.4
			31	0450	5.1
				1114	1.2
			F	1719	5.0
				2336	1.1

FEBRUARY

	Time	m		Time	m
1	0537	5.3	16	0517	5.2
	1202	0.9		1135	1.0
SA	1805	5.1	SU	1746	5.1
●			○	2354	0.9
2	0021	1.0	17	0602	5.4
	0620	5.4		1221	0.7
SU	1246	0.8	M	1831	5.2
	1847	5.1			
3	0102	0.9	18	0039	0.7
	0700	5.4		0646	5.6
M	1325	0.8	TU	1306	0.5
	1924	5.1		1913	5.3
4	0138	0.9	19	0121	0.5
	0735	5.4		0729	5.6
TU	1401	0.9	W	1347	0.4
	1957	5.1		1954	5.4
5	0211	1.0	20	0201	0.5
	0807	5.3		0810	5.6
W	1432	1.0	TH	1426	0.5
	2026	5.0		2034	5.3
6	0239	1.2	21	0239	0.6
	0837	5.1		0851	5.5
TH	1500	1.2	F	1503	0.7
	2054	4.8		2112	5.2
7	0305	1.4	22	0316	0.8
	0908	5.0		0930	5.3
F	1525	1.5	SA	1540	1.0
	2125	4.7		2151	5.0
8	0330	1.7	23	0356	1.2
	0940	4.8		1013	5.0
SA	1552	1.7	SU	1622	1.4
	2200	4.5		2235	4.7
9	0359	1.9	24	0444	1.6
	1017	4.5		1105	4.6
SU	1626	2.0	M	1714	1.8
	2242	4.3		2337	4.4
10	0443	2.2	25	0549	2.0
	1105	4.3		1222	4.3
M	1723	2.2	TU	1829	2.2
	2342	4.2			
11	0603	2.4	26	0106	4.3
	1214	4.2		0726	2.2
TU	1846	2.3	W	1355	4.2
				2022	2.2
12	0103	4.2	27	0233	4.4
	0729	2.3		0910	2.0
W	1347	4.2	TH	1516	4.4
	2003	2.2		2143	1.9
13	0232	4.4	28	0343	4.7
	0843	2.1		1015	1.5
TH	1510	4.4	F	1619	4.7
	2112	1.9		2239	1.5
14	0339	4.7			
	0948	1.7			
F	1610	4.6			
	2213	1.6			
15	0431	5.0			
	1044	1.3			
SA	1700	4.9			
	2306	1.2			

MARCH

	Time	m		Time	m
1	0437	5.0	16	0405	5.0
	1105	1.2		1023	1.2
SA	1708	4.9	SU	1638	4.9
	2325	1.1		2246	1.1
2	0522	5.2	17	0453	5.3
	1148	0.9		1114	0.8
SU	1750	5.0	M	1724	5.2
				2335	0.7
3	0005	0.9	18	0539	5.5
	0601	5.4		1201	0.4
M	1228	0.7	TU	1808	5.4
●	1826	5.1	○		
4	0043	0.7	19	0020	0.4
	0637	5.4		0624	5.7
TU	1304	0.6	W	1246	0.2
	1859	5.2		1851	5.5
5	0116	0.7	20	0102	0.3
	0710	5.4		0708	5.7
W	1336	0.7	TH	1327	0.2
	1928	5.1		1932	5.6
6	0145	0.8	21	0142	0.3
	0740	5.3		0751	5.7
TH	1403	0.9	F	1405	0.3
	1955	5.1		2012	5.5
7	0210	1.0	22	0220	0.4
	0809	5.2		0832	5.5
F	1426	1.1	SA	1442	0.6
	2023	5.0		2049	5.3
8	0230	1.2	23	0257	0.7
	0837	5.0		0911	5.3
SA	1445	1.3	SU	1519	1.0
	2050	4.8		2126	5.1
9	0249	1.4	24	0337	1.1
	0904	4.8		0953	4.9
SU	1505	1.5	M	1559	1.5
	2117	4.7		2207	4.7
10	0313	1.7	25	0424	1.6
	0932	4.5		1045	4.5
M	1531	1.8	TU	1651	2.0
	2151	4.4		2306	4.4
11	0348	2.0	26	0529	2.1
	1014	4.3		1212	4.1
TU	1613	2.1	W	1806	2.3
	2244	4.2			
12	0448	2.3	27	0049	4.2
	1122	4.1		0716	2.2
W	1743	2.4	TH	1348	4.1
				2012	2.3
13	0002	4.1	28	0219	4.4
	0646	2.4		0900	1.9
TH	1257	4.0	F	1505	4.3
	1926	2.3		2128	1.9
14	0146	4.3	29	0326	4.6
	0812	2.1		0958	1.5
F	1444	4.2	SA	1603	4.6
	2044	2.0		2219	1.5
15	0309	4.6	30	0417	4.9
	0924	1.7		1044	1.1
SA	1548	4.6	SU	1647	4.9
	2150	1.6		2302	1.1
			31	0459	5.2
				1124	0.8
			M	1724	5.1
				2341	0.9

APRIL

	Time	m		Time	m
1	0536	5.3	16	0512	5.5
	1202	0.7		1136	0.4
TU	1758	5.2	W	1741	5.5
●			○	2356	0.4
2	0016	0.7	17	0559	5.7
	0609	5.3		1220	0.2
W	1236	0.7	TH	1825	5.6
	1828	5.2			
3	0048	0.7	18	0039	0.2
	0641	5.3		0645	5.7
TH	1305	0.7	F	1303	0.2
	1857	5.2		1908	5.6
4	0116	0.8	19	0121	0.2
	0711	5.2		0730	5.6
F	1330	0.9	SA	1344	0.3
	1925	5.2		1949	5.6
5	0139	1.0	20	0201	0.4
	0741	5.1		0813	5.4
SA	1352	1.1	SU	1422	0.7
	1953	5.1		2028	5.4
6	0158	1.2	21	0241	0.8
	0808	5.0		0855	5.1
SU	1411	1.3	M	1501	1.1
	2019	4.9		2106	5.1
7	0218	1.3	22	0323	1.2
	0834	4.8		0940	4.8
M	1431	1.5	TU	1544	1.6
	2045	4.8		2148	4.8
8	0243	1.6	23	0412	1.7
	0903	4.5		1037	4.4
TU	1459	1.8	W	1637	2.0
	2118	4.6		2247	4.4
9	0319	1.9	24	0518	2.1
	0946	4.3		1205	4.1
W	1540	2.1	TH	1752	2.3
	2211	4.4			
10	0416	2.2	25	0031	4.3
	1053	4.1		0657	2.2
TH	1657	2.4	F	1330	4.1
	2324	4.2		1939	2.3
11	0613	2.3	26	0153	4.4
	1221	4.0		0829	1.9
F	1855	2.3	SA	1437	4.3
				2054	2.0
12	0057	4.3	27	0255	4.6
	0742	2.0		0925	1.6
SA	1410	4.3	SU	1530	4.6
	2015	2.0		2146	1.6
13	0231	4.6	28	0345	4.8
	0855	1.6		1011	1.2
SU	1518	4.6	M	1613	4.8
	2123	1.5		2229	1.3
14	0334	5.0	29	0426	5.0
	0956	1.1		1051	1.0
M	1609	5.0	TU	1651	5.0
	2219	1.1		2308	1.0
15	0425	5.3	30	0503	5.1
	1048	0.7		1128	0.9
TU	1656	5.3	W	1724	5.1
	2309	0.7		2344	0.9

ENGLAND — PLYMOUTH (DEVONPORT)

LAT 50°22'N LONG 4°11'W

TIME ZONE **UT(GMT)** — TIMES AND HEIGHTS OF HIGH AND LOW WATERS — YEAR **2003**

MAY

Day	Time	m	Day	Time	m
1 TH ●	0538 1201 1756	5.2 0.9 5.2	16 F ○	0535 1156 1800	5.6 0.4 5.6
2 F	0016 0611 1231 1827	0.9 5.2 0.9 5.2	17 SA	0017 0623 1241 1845	0.4 5.6 0.4 5.6
3 SA	0044 0644 1258 1857	1.0 5.1 1.0 5.2	18 **SU**	0102 0711 1324 1929	0.4 5.5 0.6 5.5
4 **SU**	0109 0716 1322 1927	1.1 5.0 1.2 5.1	19 M	0145 0756 1407 2011	0.6 5.3 0.8 5.4
5 M	0133 0746 1346 1956	1.2 4.9 1.3 5.0	20 TU	0229 0844 1449 2053	0.9 5.0 1.2 5.1
6 TU	0158 0815 1411 2025	1.4 4.7 1.5 4.9	21 W	0314 0932 1534 2136	1.2 4.7 1.6 4.8
7 W	0228 0849 1444 2102	1.5 4.6 1.7 4.7	22 TH	0404 1030 1626 2231	1.6 4.4 1.9 4.6
8 TH	0309 0935 1529 2153	1.8 4.4 2.0 4.5	23 F	0503 1142 1726 2354	1.9 4.2 2.2 4.4
9 F	0410 1037 1645 2300	2.0 4.2 2.2 4.4	24 SA	0615 1253 1844	2.0 4.2 2.2
10 SA	0545 1155 1822	2.1 4.2 2.2	25 **SU**	0110 0733 1354 1958	4.4 1.9 4.3 2.0
11 **SU**	0020 0709 1326 1941	4.5 1.9 4.3 1.9	26 M	0210 0836 1445 2057	4.5 1.7 4.5 1.8
12 M	0146 0821 1438 2049	4.7 1.5 4.7 1.5	27 TU	0301 0926 1531 2146	4.7 1.5 4.7 1.6
13 TU	0256 0923 1535 2148	5.0 1.1 5.0 1.1	28 W	0346 1010 1611 2229	4.8 1.3 4.9 1.3
14 W	0353 1018 1625 2241	5.2 0.8 5.2 0.8	29 TH	0427 1049 1648 2307	4.9 1.2 5.0 1.2
15 TH	0445 1108 1713 2330	5.4 0.5 5.4 0.5	30 F	0506 1124 1724 2342	5.0 1.1 5.1 1.1
			31 SA ●	0544 1157 1800	5.0 1.1 5.1

JUNE

Day	Time	m	Day	Time	m
1 **SU**	0014 0621 1229 1835	1.1 5.0 1.2 5.2	16 M	0047 0657 1310 1914	0.6 5.3 0.8 5.5
2 M	0046 0657 1300 1909	1.2 5.0 1.2 5.1	17 TU	0134 0746 1355 1959	0.7 5.2 0.9 5.4
3 TU	0118 0732 1332 1941	1.2 4.9 1.3 5.1	18 W	0220 0834 1439 2041	0.9 5.0 1.2 5.2
4 W	0151 0807 1405 2016	1.3 4.8 1.5 5.0	19 TH	0304 0921 1522 2123	1.1 4.8 1.4 5.0
5 TH	0228 0845 1444 2055	1.4 4.6 1.6 4.9	20 F	0349 1007 1606 2205	1.4 4.5 1.7 4.8
6 F	0312 0930 1532 2143	1.6 4.5 1.8 4.8	21 SA	0436 1057 1654 2254	1.6 4.4 1.9 4.6
7 SA	0408 1025 1633 2240	1.7 4.4 1.9 4.7	22 **SU**	0527 1153 1748 2356	1.8 4.3 2.0 4.4
8 **SU**	0517 1131 1747 2349	1.8 4.4 1.9 4.6	23 M	0624 1251 1849	1.9 4.3 2.1
9 M	0632 1244 1902	1.7 4.5 1.8	24 TU	0102 0724 1347 1951	4.4 1.9 4.3 2.0
10 TU	0104 0743 1356 2012	4.7 1.5 4.6 1.6	25 W	0204 0823 1439 2050	4.4 1.8 4.5 1.9
11 W	0218 0849 1459 2117	4.9 1.3 4.9 1.3	26 TH	0259 0917 1528 2142	4.5 1.7 4.7 1.7
12 TH	0322 0949 1556 2215	5.1 1.0 5.1 1.0	27 F	0349 1004 1614 2229	4.7 1.5 4.8 1.5
13 F	0421 1044 1649 2308	5.2 0.8 5.3 0.8	28 SA	0436 1047 1657 2311	4.8 1.4 5.0 1.4
14 SA ○	0515 1135 1739 2359	5.3 0.7 5.4 0.7	29 **SU** ●	0520 1128 1738 2350	4.9 1.3 5.1 1.3
15 **SU**	0606 1223 1827	5.3 0.7 5.5	30 M	0603 1207 1818	4.9 1.3 5.1

JULY

Day	Time	m	Day	Time	m
1 TU	0029 0643 1246 1856	1.2 4.9 1.2 5.2	16 W	0125 0733 1344 1944	0.7 5.1 0.9 5.4
2 W	0109 0724 1325 1933	1.2 4.9 1.2 5.2	17 TH	0208 0817 1424 2023	0.8 5.0 1.0 5.3
3 TH	0148 0803 1404 2010	1.2 4.9 1.3 5.1	18 F	0247 0856 1501 2058	0.9 4.9 1.2 5.1
4 F	0228 0842 1443 2049	1.2 4.8 1.3 5.1	19 SA	0324 0930 1537 2130	1.2 4.7 1.4 4.9
5 SA	0310 0923 1526 2132	1.2 4.7 1.4 5.0	20 **SU**	0400 1002 1613 2204	1.4 4.6 1.7 4.7
6 **SU**	0355 1010 1614 2221	1.3 4.6 1.5 4.9	21 M	0437 1039 1653 2246	1.7 4.4 1.9 4.5
7 M	0448 1104 1711 2319	1.5 4.6 1.7 4.8	22 TU	0521 1127 1744 2339	1.9 4.3 2.1 4.3
8 TU	0550 1207 1819	1.6 4.5 1.7	23 W	0616 1229 1846	2.1 4.2 2.2
9 W	0028 0701 1318 1935	4.7 1.6 4.6 1.7	24 TH	0050 0719 1341 1953	4.2 2.1 4.3 2.2
10 TH	0145 0816 1429 2049	4.7 1.6 4.7 1.6	25 F	0210 0823 1448 2057	4.3 2.0 4.5 2.0
11 F	0258 0925 1534 2155	4.8 1.4 4.9 1.3	26 SA	0318 0923 1545 2155	4.4 1.8 4.7 1.7
12 SA	0404 1027 1632 2255	4.9 1.2 5.1 1.1	27 **SU**	0413 1017 1634 2246	4.6 1.6 4.9 1.5
13 **SU** ○	0502 1122 1725 2348	5.1 1.0 5.3 0.9	28 M	0501 1106 1718 2332	4.8 1.4 5.1 1.2
14 M	0555 1212 1814	5.1 0.9 5.4	29 TU ●	0546 1151 1801	4.9 1.2 5.2
15 TU	0038 0645 1300 1900	0.7 5.2 0.8 5.4	30 W	0016 0629 1235 1842	1.1 5.0 1.1 5.3
			31 TH	0059 0711 1316 1922	0.9 5.0 1.0 5.3

AUGUST

Day	Time	m	Day	Time	m
1 F	0140 0752 1355 2001	0.8 5.1 0.9 5.3	16 SA	0221 0821 1433 2025	0.8 5.0 1.0 5.2
2 SA	0219 0831 1433 2039	0.8 5.0 1.0 5.3	17 **SU**	0251 0848 1501 2053	1.1 4.9 1.3 5.0
3 **SU**	0256 0909 1511 2118	0.9 5.0 1.1 5.2	18 M	0318 0915 1527 2123	1.3 4.7 1.6 4.8
4 M	0335 0949 1551 2201	1.1 4.9 1.3 5.0	19 TU	0343 0947 1553 2156	1.6 4.6 1.9 4.6
5 TU	0418 1035 1639 2251	1.3 4.7 1.5 4.8	20 W	0413 1026 1629 2239	1.9 4.4 2.1 4.3
6 W	0511 1133 1741 2357	1.6 4.6 1.8 4.6	21 TH	0502 1120 1740 2341	2.2 4.2 2.4 4.1
7 TH	0622 1247 1903	1.9 4.5 2.0	22 F	0623 1238 1906	2.4 4.2 2.4
8 F	0122 0750 1409 2033	4.4 1.9 4.5 1.9	23 SA	0120 0741 1412 2022	4.1 2.3 4.3 2.2
9 SA	0248 0914 1523 2149	4.5 1.8 4.8 1.6	24 **SU**	0254 0852 1520 2129	4.3 2.0 4.6 1.9
10 **SU**	0358 1020 1623 2249	4.7 1.5 5.0 1.2	25 M	0353 0954 1612 2225	4.6 1.7 4.9 1.5
11 M	0456 1115 1715 2341	4.9 1.1 5.3 0.9	26 TU	0442 1046 1658 2314	4.8 1.4 5.2 1.1
12 TU ○	0546 1203 1801	5.1 0.9 5.4	27 W ●	0526 1134 1741 2359	5.0 1.1 5.3 0.8
13 W	0027 0631 1246 1844	0.7 5.2 0.8 5.5	28 TH	0609 1217 1823	5.2 0.9 5.5
14 TH	0109 0713 1326 1922	0.6 5.2 0.8 5.4	29 F	0041 0651 1259 1903	0.6 5.3 0.7 5.5
15 F	0147 0750 1401 1956	0.7 5.1 0.8 5.3	30 SA	0122 0731 1338 1943	0.5 5.3 0.6 5.6
			31 **SU**	0200 0810 1415 2022	0.6 5.3 0.7 5.5

ENGLAND — PLYMOUTH (DEVONPORT)

LAT 50°22′N LONG 4°11′W

TIME ZONE UT(GMT) — TIMES AND HEIGHTS OF HIGH AND LOW WATERS — YEAR 2003

SEPTEMBER

Day	Time	m	Day	Time	m
1 M	0236	0.7	16 TU	0233	1.4
	0847	5.2		0835	4.9
	1451	0.9		1440	1.5
	2100	5.3		2045	4.9
2 TU	0312	1.0	17 W	0251	1.6
	0925	5.1		0904	4.7
	1529	1.2		1458	1.8
	2140	5.1		2114	4.6
3 W	0351	1.4	18 TH	0311	1.9
	1008	4.8		0939	4.5
	1613	1.6		1527	2.1
	2227	4.7		2152	4.3
4 TH	0441	1.8	19 F	0346	2.2
	1103	4.5		1028	4.3
	1714	2.0		1618	2.4
	2335	4.4		2253	4.1
5 F	0552	2.2	20 SA	0506	2.6
	1227	4.4		1141	4.2
	1846	2.2		1825	2.6
6 SA	0118	4.2	21 SU	0026	4.0
	0744	2.3		0706	2.5
	1402	4.4		1329	4.3
	2036	2.1		1952	2.3
7 SU	0250	4.4	22 M	0231	4.2
	0915	2.0		0825	2.2
	1518	4.7		1453	4.6
	2148	1.6		2104	1.9
8 M	0358	4.7	23 TU	0332	4.6
	1014	1.5		0930	1.8
	1616	5.0		1546	5.0
	2241	1.2		2201	1.4
9 TU	0449	5.0	24 W	0419	4.9
	1103	1.1		1023	1.3
	1702	5.3		1632	5.3
	2327	0.9		2250	1.0
10 W	0531	5.1	25 TH	0502	5.2
	1146	0.9		1110	1.0
	1743	5.5		1715	5.5
○				2335	0.7
11 TH	0008	0.7	26 F	0544	5.4
	0609	5.2		1154	0.7
	1225	0.7		1758	5.6
	1820	5.5	●		
12 F	0046	0.6	27 SA	0018	0.5
	0644	5.3		0624	5.5
	1301	0.7		1236	0.5
	1854	5.5		1839	5.7
13 SA	0119	0.7	28 SU	0059	0.4
	0715	5.2		0705	5.5
	1332	0.8		1316	0.5
	1923	5.4		1921	5.7
14 SU	0149	0.8	29 M	0137	0.5
	0742	5.2		0745	5.5
	1400	1.0		1354	0.6
	1951	5.3		2002	5.6
15 M	0213	1.1	30 TU	0214	0.7
	0808	5.1		0824	5.4
	1422	1.3		1431	0.9
	2018	5.1		2041	5.3

OCTOBER

Day	Time	m	Day	Time	m
1 W	0250	1.1	16 TH	0212	1.7
	0903	5.2		0831	4.9
	1510	1.2		1425	1.8
	2122	5.0		2043	4.6
2 TH	0330	1.5	17 F	0235	1.9
	0945	4.9		0905	4.7
	1556	1.7		1456	2.1
	2211	4.6		2123	4.4
3 F	0420	2.0	18 SA	0311	2.2
	1042	4.6		0953	4.4
	1700	2.2		1544	2.4
	2329	4.2		2224	4.1
4 SA	0538	2.4	19 SU	0412	2.6
	1217	4.4		1102	4.3
	1847	2.4		1743	2.6
				2348	4.0
5 SU	0121	4.2	20 M	0630	2.6
	0744	2.4		1232	4.3
	1354	4.5		1919	2.3
	2032	2.1			
6 M	0246	4.4	21 TU	0150	4.2
	0903	2.0		0752	2.3
	1505	4.8		1411	4.6
	2133	1.6		2031	1.9
7 TU	0346	4.7	22 W	0259	4.6
	0956	1.6		0858	1.8
	1558	5.1		1511	5.0
	2221	1.2		2129	1.4
8 W	0430	5.0	23 TH	0348	5.0
	1040	1.2		0953	1.4
	1641	5.3		1600	5.3
	2302	0.9		2220	1.0
9 TH	0507	5.2	24 F	0432	5.3
	1120	0.9		1042	1.0
	1718	5.4		1646	5.5
	2341	0.8		2307	0.7
10 F	0541	5.3	25 SA	0515	5.5
	1157	0.8		1128	0.7
	1752	5.5		1731	5.7
○			●	2351	0.5
11 SA	0015	0.7	26 SU	0558	5.6
	0612	5.4		1211	0.5
	1231	0.8		1816	5.8
	1823	5.4			
12 SU	0047	0.8	27 M	0033	0.4
	0640	5.3		0640	5.7
	1300	0.9		1254	0.5
	1851	5.4		1900	5.7
13 M	0113	1.0	28 TU	0115	0.6
	0707	5.3		0722	5.7
	1325	1.1		1335	0.6
	1919	5.2		1943	5.5
14 TU	0135	1.2	29 W	0154	0.8
	0735	5.2		0804	5.5
	1346	1.3		1416	0.9
	1947	5.1		2027	5.3
15 W	0154	1.4	30 TH	0234	1.2
	0803	5.1		0846	5.3
	1404	1.6		1459	1.3
	2015	4.9		2112	4.9
			31 F	0317	1.7
				0931	5.0
				1549	1.8
				2206	4.6

NOVEMBER

Day	Time	m	Day	Time	m
1 SA	0411	2.1	16 SU	0259	2.1
	1031	4.7		0933	4.6
	1654	2.2		1537	2.2
	2330	4.3		2206	4.3
2 SU	0527	2.4	17 M	0400	2.4
	1203	4.5		1034	4.5
	1832	2.3		1704	2.3
				2318	4.2
3 M	0105	4.2	18 TU	0543	2.5
	0716	2.4		1148	4.5
	1330	4.5		1837	2.2
	2003	2.1			
4 TU	0218	4.4	19 W	0047	4.3
	0831	2.1		0710	2.3
	1435	4.8		1312	4.7
	2102	1.7		1950	1.9
5 W	0314	4.7	20 TH	0208	4.6
	0924	1.7		0819	1.9
	1527	5.0		1425	4.9
	2149	1.4		2052	1.5
6 TH	0358	5.0	21 F	0308	4.9
	1008	1.4		0919	1.5
	1610	5.2		1524	5.2
	2231	1.2		2148	1.1
7 F	0435	5.2	22 SA	0359	5.2
	1048	1.2		1012	1.1
	1647	5.3		1616	5.4
	2308	1.0		2239	0.8
8 SA	0509	5.3	23 SU	0447	5.5
	1125	1.1		1102	0.8
	1721	5.3		1706	5.6
	2342	1.0	●	2326	0.7
9 SU	0540	5.3	24 M	0533	5.6
	1159	1.0		1149	0.7
	1753	5.3		1755	5.6
○					
10 M	0012	1.0	25 TU	0012	0.6
	0609	5.4		0619	5.7
	1229	1.1		1236	0.6
	1823	5.3		1843	5.6
11 TU	0040	1.2	26 W	0057	0.7
	0639	5.3		0704	5.7
	1255	1.3		1321	0.7
	1855	5.2		1930	5.4
12 W	0104	1.3	27 TH	0140	1.0
	0710	5.3		0750	5.6
	1319	1.4		1406	1.0
	1925	5.0		2018	5.2
13 TH	0127	1.5	28 F	0225	1.3
	0740	5.1		0836	5.4
	1343	1.6		1453	1.3
	1955	4.9		2108	4.9
14 F	0151	1.7	29 SA	0311	1.6
	0811	5.0		0924	5.1
	1410	1.8		1543	1.6
	2028	4.7		2203	4.6
15 SA	0220	1.9	30 SU	0402	2.0
	0846	4.8		1020	4.8
	1446	2.0		1641	1.9
	2109	4.5		2310	4.4

DECEMBER

Day	Time	m	Day	Time	m
1 M	0503	2.2	16 TU	0351	2.0
	1131	4.6		1011	4.8
	1750	2.1		1633	2.0
				2249	4.4
2 TU	0024	4.3	17 W	0457	2.1
	0618	2.3		1112	4.7
	1245	4.6		1745	2.0
	1906	2.1		2357	4.4
3 W	0130	4.4	18 TH	0616	2.1
	0735	2.2		1221	4.7
	1348	4.6		1901	1.9
	2013	1.9			
4 TH	0226	4.6	19 F	0111	4.6
	0837	2.0		0733	1.9
	1442	4.8		1336	4.8
	2106	1.7		2011	1.7
5 F	0314	4.8	20 SA	0223	4.8
	0928	1.8		0842	1.7
	1530	4.9		1446	5.0
	2151	1.6		2116	1.4
6 SA	0357	4.9	21 SU	0326	5.0
	1012	1.6		0945	1.4
	1612	5.0		1550	5.2
	2231	1.4		2214	1.2
7 SU	0434	5.1	22 M	0422	5.3
	1051	1.4		1041	1.1
	1650	5.1		1647	5.3
	2308	1.3		2307	1.0
8 M	0509	5.2	23 TU	0514	5.5
	1128	1.3		1134	0.9
	1727	5.1		1740	5.4
○	2341	1.3	●	2357	0.9
9 TU	0544	5.3	24 W	0604	5.6
	1201	1.3		1224	0.8
	1803	5.1		1832	5.4
10 W	0012	1.3	25 TH	0046	0.9
	0619	5.3		0652	5.6
	1233	1.4		1313	0.8
	1838	5.1		1922	5.3
11 TH	0043	1.4	26 F	0133	0.9
	0654	5.3		0741	5.6
	1304	1.4		1400	0.9
	1913	5.0		2012	5.2
12 F	0114	1.5	27 SA	0218	1.1
	0728	5.2		0827	5.5
	1336	1.5		1446	1.0
	1948	4.9		2059	5.0
13 SA	0145	1.6	28 SU	0301	1.3
	0801	5.1		0912	5.3
	1410	1.6		1530	1.3
	2023	4.8		2145	4.8
14 SU	0220	1.7	29 M	0344	1.6
	0837	5.0		0956	5.0
	1448	1.7		1615	1.6
	2103	4.6		2231	4.6
15 M	0301	1.9	30 TU	0429	1.8
	0920	4.9		1042	4.8
	1535	1.9		1702	1.8
	2151	4.5		2321	4.4
			31 W	0520	2.1
				1134	4.6
				1755	2.0

Advertisers by Category

See Index of Advertisers on page 68 for page numbers.

Attractions
National Maritime Museum (Cornwall)

Bars and Restaurant
Salcombe Coffee Company
Mountbatten Centre

Batteries
Marco Marine
Mountbatten Boathouse
Yacht Parts Plymouth

Boat Building, Repairing and Lay Up
Boating World
Bridgend Boat Company
Fast Tack yachts
Lynher Boatyard
Mayflower Marina
Plymouth Yacht Haven
Rocky Pindar Boatyard
Shore Store
Starey Marine Services
Weir Quay Boatyard
Yeowards Boatyard

Boats Sales and Brokerage
Ancasta Plymouth
Barbican Yacht Agency
Boating World
Lynher Boatyard
Watkin Boat Sales
Westways of Plymouth
Weir Quay Boatyard
Yeowards Boatyard

Inflatable Boats
Danby Marime Safety
Inflatable Boat Services

Books and Charts
Sea Chest, The
Weir Quay Boatyard

Chandlers
Marine Bazaar
Mountbatten Boathouse
Weir Quay Boatyard
Yacht Parts Plymouth

Clothes - Casual and Formal
Watkin Boat Sales

Clothing- Sailing and Recreational
Marine Bazzaar
Mountbatten Boathouse
Watkin Boat Sales
Yacht Parts Plymouth

Cycle Hire
Plymouth Cycle Hire

Electronic Equipment
Marco Marine
Seacom Electronics
Waypoint 1, Marine Electronics

Marinas
Falmouth Harbour Commissioners
Mayflower Marina
Mylor Yacht Harbour Ltd.
Shore Store
Plymouth Yacht Haven
Port Pendennis Marina

Marine Engines & Engineers
Boating World
Bridgend Boat Company
Lynher Boatyard

Marco Marine
Starey Marine
Western Marine Power
Weir Boatyard
Yeowards Boatyard

Metals and Fastenings
Aqua-tech Marine
Phoenix 316 Ltd
Stainless Steel Centre

Mooring
Boating World
Lynher Boatyard
Rocky Pindar Boatyard
Shore Store
Weir Quay Boatyard
Yeowards Boatyard

Gifts
Salcombe Chocolate Factory

Outboard Motors- Sales and Services
Inflatable Boat Services
Marco Marine
Mountbatten Boathouse
Watkin Boat Sales
Yeowards Boatyard

Rigging Services
Allspars
Eurospars
Yacht Rigging Services

Safety Equipment
Danby Maritime Safety

Sails & Covers
Inshore Sails and Covers
Osens Sails Ltd.

Sailing Schools and Yacht Charters
Plymouth Sailing School
Westways of Plymouth

Stainless Steelwork
Aqua-tech
Phoenix 316

Telecommunications Equipment
Seacom Electronics
Waypoint 1, Plymouth

Tuition
Mountbatten Centre

Wooden Yacht Building & Repairs
Bridgend Boat Company

Yacht Brokerage
Ancasta Plymouth
Westways of Plymouth
Yeowards Boatyard

Index of Advertisers

NATIONAL COASTWATCH INSTITUTION
NCI *Looking out for you*

We're there to help you …
Each station is manned in daylight hours 365 days a year to watch out for sea and coastal users

It all started in 1994 when two Cornish fishermen lost their lives close to the recently closed Bass Point coast guard station. A group of local people decided to set up an organisation to restore *visual watch* along the UK coast. With the opening of Bass Point station, the National Coastwatch Institution was born. It is a registered charity. By early 2002 there were 23 stations operating. Not only do they keep visual lookout, the operators can give information on up-to-the-minute local conditions

Photo: Joan Gross, NCI

before yachtsmen and fishermen ever leave harbour. All of the volunteer operators are trained and must know how to deal with any emergency. Each station is responsible for its own funding, equipment, maintenance of their station and training of watch keepers. Operators come from all walks of life, but have one thing in common, they are firm believers in preventing loss of life. Please donate to keep this voluntary service operating in your area.

NCI operators report many life-threatening incidents to HM Coastguard, the co-ordinators of all Search and Rescue operations in UK waters. The watch keepers observe and record what is happening on their patch and pass on the relevant information to the appropriate authority. A capsized boat can easily lose communication and it is only the human eye can pick up a distress flare out at sea. Windsurfers, swimmers, canoeists and divers can be swept out to sea in strong winds with no way of communicating if a tragedy occurs. Coastal walkers, bird watchers, and even dogs and sheep can get into difficulties in bad weather.

Can you help us?
Please return this form with a donation, however small, to the address below.

To: The Secretary, NCI Prawle Point, Kingsbridge, Devon TQ7 2ES
Name: Title:
Address:
Post Code:
• (tick the box) I would like to become a supporter of NCI Prawle Point by donating
£____________ *(cheques made out to NCI Prawle Point)*
• (tick the box) Gift Aid, I would like the National Coastwatch Institution to treat my donation as Gift Aid.
I will have paid income/capital gains tax at least equal to the amount the charity will reclaim on my donation.

Signed:______________________ Date:________________

Print name:____